Beach Appétit

THE JUNIOR LEAGUE *of the* EMERALD COAST

Beach Appétit

Published by the Junior League of
the Emerald Coast, Inc.

Copyright © 2004 by
The Junior League of the Emerald Coast, Inc.
Post Office Box 531
Fort Walton Beach, Florida 32549
850-862-2665

This cookbook is a collection of
favorite recipes, which are not
necessarily original recipes.

Library of Congress Control Number: 2003110324
ISBN: 0-9741258-0-6

Edited, Designed, and Manufactured by
Favorite Recipes® Press
an Imprint of

FRP

P.O. Box 305142
Nashville, Tennessee 37230
800-358-0560

Art Director: Steve Newman
Book Design: Jim Scott
Project Editor: Jane Hinshaw
Project Manager: Tanis Westbrook

Manufactured in the United States of America
First Printing: 2004
15,000 copies

Photography provided by Dill Beaty

Patrons

Thank you to the following individuals and businesses,
who have given their generous financial support to *Beach Appétit*:

Albertson's

Kristen Pope

Cox Communications

Destin Bank

Ruckel Properties

SPECIAL ACKNOWLEDGMENTS

A special thank-you to the following, who
contributed their time, talent, possessions,
or locale for our photography:

Chef Jason Knoll

Cover Stories

Bonnie and Butch Smith

Randy and Julia Roark

John Ridgeway at Waterview Towers

Aunt Martha's Bed and Breakfast

Galati Yacht Sales

Eden State Park

Dill and Julie Beaty

COMMITTEE 2002–2003

Claire Benz

Bonnie Bianca

Julie Dubuisson Cotton

Nancy Davis

Jennifer Esses

Erin Hansen

Karen Morris

Peggy Nehring

Melodie Phillips

Gretchen Severance

Sarah Smith

Jennifer Stennett

Anita Turner

Kefrin Woodham

Preface

The Junior League of the Emerald Coast began in February 1965 due to the vision of five women residing in Fort Walton Beach. President Sug Brown, Barbara Smith, Carolyn Crotzer, Boota Walker, and B.J. Totten recognized the need for volunteerism in our local area, and what better way to get that started than a service organization based on the fellowship of dynamic women. The group quickly grew and eventually joined the Association of Junior Leagues International in 1987. In January 2000, the name of our organization was changed to Junior League of the Emerald Coast to reflect the widening spectrum of membership and community involvement. Currently, our membership boasts over 150 active members consisting of a diverse group of educated and spirited women. We are professionals and stay-at-home mothers. We are single and married. We are accountants, doctors, lawyers, schoolteachers, designers, marketing reps, and real estate agents. In short, we represent every segment of our growing community. It is our vision to be recognized as a leader in our community for volunteerism, and we strive to do that by developing the potential of our members and effectively training them as volunteers through our organization's signature projects.

Each year, the Junior League of the Emerald Coast participates in a wide variety of community service projects primarily geared at improving the lives of other women and children in the greater Fort Walton Beach area. In partnership with other community service organizations, such as the Niceville Children's Advocacy Center, Habitat for Humanity, Florida Department of Children and Families, and Sharing & Caring, we have effectively made a difference in this community. Annually, we clothe over 250 needy children through the Child Clothing Project. In conjunction with the Okaloosa and Walton County School Districts, needy children are identified, taken to local stores, and provided with a shopping bag and the means to pick out brand-new clothing. With shopping complete, children gather for lunch. The day is capped off with volunteers and children leaving with full hearts after a day of emotional outreach. Other projects include a program called "Suit Up to Move Up," which allows women attempting to gain entry into the workforce without the financial means to purchase interview clothing the chance to come to a stocked closet and choose an outfit. One of our newest projects, "Totes for Tots and Teens," allows children who are removed from their families to have new suitcases to move with that are filled with the essentials they might need for their first few nights in new surroundings.

Over the years, we have physically changed the landscape of our town by renovating historic landmarks, including the Camp Walton Schoolhouse, Garnier's Post Office, and most recently, the historic Gulfview Hotel, all doomed for destruction without the League's intervention.

The Junior League of the Emerald Coast obtains the funding for these and other projects through our annual fund-raising endeavors. These include the sale of this cookbook, our spring gala, "Emerald Evening," the sale of gift-wrap, spring/fall charity sales, and other volunteer efforts. Proceeds from the sale of *Beach Appétit* will go directly to their support and will allow the League to continue having a significant impact in our community and the lives of local women and children.

Introduction

Beach Appétit is the second cookbook from the Junior League of the Emerald Coast. Our last cookbook, *Sugar Beach*, completely sold out. This told us it was time to get back to the drawing board, or the cupboard as the case may be, and start working on some new recipes.

With its beautiful coastline and emerald green waters, the Emerald Coast is a wonderful place to live, and it is no wonder that seafood plays a large role in the local cuisine. One only has to stand on the dock in Destin or glance over the Mid-Bay Bridge in the early evening to see the countless fishing trawlers to realize the impact that seafood has on our economy and appetites. The majority of our finest dining establishments are situated along the Gulf and heavily feature local seafood, such as amberjack, snapper, cobia, tuna, crab, and shrimp on their menus. It is referred to as "coastal cuisine."

The focus of *Beach Appétit* is to provide a flavor of the Emerald Coast area and attractions, particularly those featuring wine and food. Within the pages of this cookbook, you will find sidebars describing our local seafood and food and wine festivals. *Beach Appétit* will provide information on some of the best dining establishments in our area, as well as go into depth about several of the local fish and agricultural products that make up coastal cuisine. The members of the Junior League of the Emerald Coast share with you our favorite recipes, tested in our own kitchens, highlighting the best foods our region has to offer. We invite you to turn the pages and take a culinary journey along the Emerald Coast of Florida. Bon *Beach Appétit*!

Contents

Symbols are used throughout *Beach Appétit* to designate the following:

Best of *Sugar Beach* Recipes

Food Preparation Information

Beverage Information

Botanical or Produce Information

Junior League of the Emerald Coast Information

Local History

Festivals

Area Activities

Menus

Entertaining is an art. No two meals are ever the same, despite the recipes on the table. Here, we have suggested menus to delight the special people who grace your table, whether that table is an inlaid walnut antique or a bamboo tray by the pool.

Because lives today are so busy, we have provided some flexibility in menu options. Each theme has one suggested menu for times when you can plan ahead and make more extensive preparations. Another gives you alternatives for fare that is quicker to assemble when time is at a premium. Our hope is that special meals will enrich your days. Good food and good friends are the magic of life.

Cocktails and Cheese Bites

Head to the deli first for these fun and quirky cocktail party menu ingredients. Boasting a wide range of cheeses, this menu selection offers the versatility of a favorite ingredient in diverse and colorful presentations. Add the trendy Cosmos and dessert martinis, and you have a fun and pleasing assortment in which everyone will discover a new favorite.

PLAN AHEAD			LAST MINUTE
Cosmopolitans with Infused Vodkas	40	40	Cosmopolitans
Marinated Cheese Trio	16	33	Hot Pecan Dip
Cajun-Style Won Tons	19	34	Crab Meat Butter
Stuffed Snow Peas	22	24	Olive Crostini
Crab Island Cheesecake	26	18	Bleu Cheese-Stuffed Mushrooms
Chocolate Royale and White Chocolate Dessert Martinis	37	37	Chocolate Royale and White Chocolate Dessert Martinis

Holiday Sideboard of Sweets

Amid the whirlwind of holiday celebrations, set aside an evening to have your neighbors and friends over for a decadent display of dessert selections. No one can resist "just a bite" of these delicacies. Extend an invitation to them to join your traditional holiday event, whether that is the preschool play, the Nutcracker ballet, or driving through the streets to see the light displays. Round out the evening with some festive music and the divine tastes offered here.

PLAN AHEAD			LAST MINUTE
Olde-Tyme Eggnog	36	44	Coffees Around the World
Four Fudge Bundt Cake	197	205	Chocolate Chess Pie
Strawberry Cream Angel Food Cake	204	190	Strawberry Blitz Torte
Praline Carrot Cake	202	192	Almond Madeleines
Rich and Creamy Cheesecake	194	187	Peaches and Cream

Grecian Heritage Feast

Inspired by Destin's Greek shipbuilding past and the growth that evolved from that endeavor, this menu highlights the Mediterranean influence on coastal cuisine. Start with the freshest of ingredients, and you can be assured of a superb meal that illustrates why Destin is nicknamed "The World's Luckiest Fishing Village."

PLAN AHEAD			LAST MINUTE
Spanakopita with Greek Salsa	25	24	Spinach and Feta Crostini
Skewered Rosemary Lamb on Couscous with Curried Oil	141	161	Greek Spaghetti with Tomatoes and Feta
Pita Bread	71	105	Mediterranean Grouper
Greek-Style Zucchini	174	164	Char-grilled Artichokes
Chocolate Flan	185	189	Navel Orange Tart

The Krewe's All Here

From Billy Bowlegs to Fat Tuesday, the Emerald Coast loves an excuse for a big parade. These Cajun-inspired selections are the perfect meal to serve before venturing out to festivities, or use them for a spiced-up dinner party whenever the pirate or jester within calls for a good time!

PLAN AHEAD			LAST MINUTE
Pirate Punch	43	43	Destin Boat Punch
Cajun Egg Rolls	17	116	Scalloped Oysters
Crawfish Bisque	77	119	Cajun Shrimp
Bahama Bayou Chicken	148	159	Jambalaya Pasta
Cajun Red Beans and Rice Salad	94	171	Spicy Whole Okra
Bread Pudding with Vanilla Sauce	186	215	Pralines
Praline Coffee	45		Coffee

A Reason to Celebrate!

Sometimes life just calls for celebration! Life-changing events chime out for an elegant gathering of loved ones to wish one well. Break out the elegant china, and host this midday meal to celebrate a new baby's baptism, a child's graduation, or a special birthday or anniversary. It works equally well as a buffet reception or a seated meal. The next time you have the inclination to host a baby shower or bridesmaids' luncheon, let this menu be your guide.

PLAN AHEAD				LAST MINUTE
Oh My, Junior League Punch	42		41	Refreshing Cranberry Blush
Seviche	22		21	Shrimp Flambé
Berries Go Tropical Salad	88		99	Spring Greens with Tomato Basil Dressing
Lemon and Herb Roasted Chicken	149		50	Spinach and Prosciutto Frittata
Roasted Asparagus	166		200	Glazed Lemon Pound Cake
Strawberry Blitz Torte	190			

Romantic Rendezvous

Sunset moments on a blanket by the water are a welcome respite for vacationers and natives alike. Whether it's a few stolen moments without the children or just a break from the daily grind, hearing the waves break on the sand and feeling the breeze in your hair can remind you why the beach is a favorite destination year after year. Chill a beverage and pack a basket for an evening under the stars.

PLAN AHEAD				LAST MINUTE
Grapefruit Margaritas	39		41	Sustainer Punch
Olive Bites	23		28	Pineapple Cheese Ball
Chicken Fruit Salad	98		146	Summer Grilled Chicken Wraps
on Crescent Rolls	66			(hold the onions)
Tiramisu	191		213	Sugar Beach Cookies

He's Gone Fishing

Send him off in style on that all-day charter. Pack these items in the cooler with some ice the night before, and prepare to sleep in. His friends won't know whether to admire him more for his fresh catch or scrumptious lunch! He will be so happy when he gets home that he'll handle dinner.

PLAN AHEAD			LAST MINUTE
Seaside Shrimp Dip	33	18	Tex-Mex Deviled Eggs
Caper Steak Salad Sandwich	84	138	Three Meat Loaf Sandwich
Fresh Vegetable Potato Salad	92	91	Cucumber Slaw
Brownies with Chocolate Chip Cheesecake Topping	209	212	Candy Cookies

Sunbathing and Sangria

While your mate is at sea or on the links, whip up these tempting treats, and have the girls over for a day by the pool or on the beach. Whether you choose the menu items to cool you down or spice it up, you will be the diva of the day!

PLAN AHEAD			LAST MINUTE
White Sangria	41	41	Garden Sangria
Mushroom Pâté	27	29	Black Bean and Corn Salsa with Chips
Chilled Avocado and Cucumber Soup	83	176	Roasted Pepper Rice
Fish Tacos	102	121	Mexican Shrimp
Kahlúa Cake	199	211	Cinnamon Crisps

Marinated Cheese Trio

Confetti Marinade

1/2 cup olive oil
1/2 cup red wine vinegar
1/4 cup fresh lime juice
1 teaspoon sugar
1/2 teaspoon salt

1/2 teaspoon freshly ground pepper
1/2 cup drained and chopped roasted
   red bell peppers
3 green onions with stems, minced
3 tablespoons chopped parsley

Cheese

1 (8-ounce) block sharp Cheddar cheese
1 (8-ounce) block Pepper Jack cheese

1 (8-ounce) package cream cheese
1/4 cup sliced kalamata olives

To *prepare the marinade*, combine the olive oil, vinegar and lime juice in a bowl and whisk until smooth. Whisk in the sugar, salt and pepper. Add the roasted peppers, green onions and parsley and mix well.

To *prepare the cheese*, cut the block of Cheddar cheese into halves lengthwise. Cut the halves crosswise into 1/4-inch slices. Repeat with the Pepper Jack cheese and cream cheese.

Stand the cheese slices on edge to form a log in a shallow dish lined with plastic wrap, alternating the cheeses. Spoon the marinade over the top. Marinate, covered, in the refrigerator for 8 hours or longer.

Remove the log to a serving plate using the plastic wrap to hold the log together. Remove the plastic wrap. Spoon some of the marinade over the top. Sprinkle with the olives and serve with assorted crackers.

Serves 6 to 8

COCKTAIL FOOD

When hosting a cocktail party, you should estimate two to two and one-half pieces of each savory item for each person and a total of twelve pieces for each person. At a cocktail party for thirty to fifty people, serve five or six different appetizers. For larger parties, you will need seven or eight choices. Always begin with vegetarian items, such as a cheese board and a crudité platter. When estimating cheese, calculate one ounce per person. Always plan on serving larger amounts of favorite items, such as prawns or oysters on the half shell. If you choose to serve desserts, opt for bite-size choices so guests can help themselves to tiny portions, especially if there are several options.

Cajun Chicken Egg Rolls with Creole Mustard Sauce

Creole Mustard Sauce

2 cups mayonnaise
1/4 cup Creole mustard
1/4 cup prepared mustard
1 tablespoon German herbed
   wine vinegar
1 tablespoon Champagne vinegar
1 tablespoon Worcestershire sauce

2 tablespoons horseradish
Tabasco sauce to taste
cayenne pepper to taste
1 green onion, chopped
1 rib celery, chopped
1/4 medium onion, chopped
1/4 red bell pepper, chopped

Egg Rolls

4 boneless skinless chicken breasts
1 teaspoon Cajun seasoning
3 tablespoons olive oil
3 garlic cloves, minced
1 head napa cabbage, finely chopped
2 (8-ounce) cans water chestnuts

1 carrot
2 (10-ounce) packages frozen corn
1 (10-ounce) can beef broth
salt, pepper and Cajun seasoning
2 (12-count) packages egg roll wrappers
vegetable oil for deep-frying

To prepare the sauce, combine the mayonnaise, Creole mustard, yellow mustard, vinegars, Worcestershire sauce, horseradish, Tabasco sauce and cayenne pepper in a food processor and process to mix well. Add the green onion, celery, onion and bell pepper and process until smooth. Spoon into a serving bowl. Store in the refrigerator until serving time.

To prepare the egg rolls, trim the chicken and pound with a meat mallet. Season with 1 teaspoon Cajun seasoning. Sauté in 1 tablespoon of the olive oil in a skillet. Drain and chop the chicken.

Heat the remaining 2 tablespoons olive oil in a clean skillet and add the garlic and cabbage. Sauté until the cabbage is tender. Process the water chestnuts and carrot in a food processor to chop. Add to the cabbage. Add the corn and beef broth and mix well. Season with salt, pepper and additional Cajun seasoning. Add the chicken and simmer until heated through. Spoon into a colander and drain.

Spoon the chicken mixture onto the egg roll wrappers and roll the wrappers to enclose the filling; moisten the edges with water or a small amount of oil and press to seal. Deep-fry in heated vegetable oil until golden brown. Serve with the mustard sauce.

Serves 12

The photograph for this recipe appears on page 14.

Tex-Mex Deviled Eggs

6 hard-cooked eggs
1 tablespoon chopped green onions
1 tablespoon finely chopped cilantro
1 small jalapeño chile, seeded and
    finely chopped
1/4 cup mayonnaise

1 teaspoon prepared mustard
1/2 teaspoon salt
1/4 cup (1 ounce) shredded
    Cheddar cheese
chile powder to taste

Cut the eggs into halves and remove the yolks to a bowl, reserving the whites. Mash the yolks until smooth. Add the green onions, cilantro, jalapeño chile, mayonnaise, mustard and salt and mix well. Spoon the mixture back into the egg whites and top with the cheese and chile powder. Arrange on a serving plate.

Serves 6

Bleu Cheese-Stuffed Mushrooms

14 to 16 (2-inch) cremini and/or
    button mushrooms
4 green onions, sliced
1 garlic clove, minced

2 tablespoons butter
1/2 cup (2 ounces) crumbled bleu cheese
1/3 cup toasted pine nuts
2 tablespoons chopped flat-leaf parsley

Remove and chop the mushroom stems; stems should measure about 1 cup. Sauté the stems with the green onions and garlic in the butter in a skillet over medium heat for 5 minutes or until tender. Remove from the heat and stir in the cheese, pine nuts and parsley.

    Spoon the sautéed mixture into the mushroom caps and arrange in a 10×15-inch baking pan. Bake at 400 degrees for 12 to 15 minutes or until the mushroom caps are tender.

Makes 14 to 16

Cajun-Style Won Tons

4 slices bacon, chopped
2 ribs celery, chopped
2 onions, chopped
1 green bell pepper, chopped
2 garlic cloves, chopped
1 teaspoon cayenne pepper, or to taste
2 cups finely chopped fresh or frozen
   crawfish tails

1 cup (4 ounces) shredded
   Cheddar cheese
1 cup (4 ounces) grated Romano cheese
26 won ton wrappers
1 egg, beaten
vegetable oil for deep-frying

Sauté the bacon in a skillet. Add the celery, onions and bell pepper and sauté until tender. Stir in the garlic and cayenne pepper. Add the crawfish and sauté briefly. Remove from the heat and let stand until cool. Stir in the Cheddar cheese and Romano cheese.

Spoon the mixture onto the won ton wrappers. Roll the wrappers to enclose the filling. Brush the edges with the egg and press to seal. Deep-fry in heated vegetable oil for 3 minutes or until light brown; drain.

Makes 26

PINE NUTS

Pine nuts, also known as pignoli, are small ivory-colored seeds extracted from the cones of a species of pine tree. They are appreciated for their rich, slightly resinous flavor. Pine nuts are used whole as an ingredient or as a garnish, or they can be puréed to use as a thickener. They are excellent in pesto, sauces, and pastries.

Oysters Rockefeller

1 cup (2 sticks) butter
1/4 cup finely chopped celery
1/4 cup finely chopped shallots
    or scallions
4 garlic cloves, finely minced
1/3 cup chopped fennel bulb
1 tablespoon chopped fennel leaves
2 cups chopped watercress leaves
1/3 cup finely chopped parsley
1/4 cup sambuca or other
    anise-flavored liqueur
salt and freshly ground pepper
    to taste
rock salt
2 dozen oysters on the half shell

Heat the butter in a skillet. Add the celery, shallots, garlic and fennel bulb and sauté until the celery and fennel are tender. Add the fennel leaves, watercress and parsley and sauté for several minutes or just until the watercress wilts. Remove to a blender or food processor. Add the liqueur, salt and pepper and process until smooth. Spoon into a bowl and chill, covered, until serving time.

Place a thick layer of rock salt in a baking pan and arrange the oysters on the half shell in the salt. Spoon 1 teaspoon of the watercress sauce on each oyster. Bake at 450 degrees for 4 minutes or until the sauce is bubbly and the edges of the oysters curl.

You can also grill the oysters. Place the oysters in the shells directly on the grill, place a dollop of sauce on each one and grill until the sauce is bubbly and deep green. The sauce can be frozen for several months.

Serves 6

Shrimp Flambé

16 jumbo Gulf shrimp, peeled
   and deveined
16 fresh basil leaves
16 slices prosciutto

3 tablespoons butter
½ cup finely chopped shallots
⅔ cup Grand Marnier or tequila
sliced cantaloupe

Wrap each shrimp in a basil leaf and then in a slice of prosciutto; secure with a wooden pick if necessary. Melt half the butter in a large skillet. Add half the shallots and sauté over medium heat for 3 to 4 minutes or until tender. Add half the shrimp and sauté for 30 seconds on each side or until the prosciutto is a roasted orange color.

Add half the Grand Marnier and swirl it around the pan. Remove from the heat and ignite with a match. Return to the heat and cook until the flames subside. Cook until the liquid is reduced to a syrupy consistency. Remove to a bowl and keep warm.

Repeat the process with the remaining half of the ingredients. Combine with the shrimp in the bowl. Serve with sliced cantaloupe.

You may also spoon the shrimp over risotto to serve as a main dish.

Serves 8

DEVEINING SHRIMP

Use a skewer to devein shrimp, either in the shell or peeled, for the most attractive presentation. Insert a thin sharp skewer crosswise beneath the vein and gently pull it out. If the vein should break, reinsert the skewer above or below the break and repeat the process. If the appearance of the shrimp is less important, you can devein peeled shrimp by making a shallow cut lengthwise down the back of the shrimp and rinsing out the vein.

Stuffed Snow Peas

50 snow pea pods
salt to taste
8 quarts water
12 ounces cooked lump crab meat
1/2 large red bell pepper, finely chopped

4 ribs celery, finely chopped
2 tablespoons chopped parsley
1/4 cup mayonnaise
3 tablespoons lemon juice
pepper to taste

String the pea pods and split open along the curved side. Bring the salted water to a boil in a large stockpot. Add the snow peas and blanch for 20 seconds. Plunge immediately into cold water in a large bowl to halt the cooking process. Drain and pat dry.

Flake the crab meat and combine with the bell pepper, celery, parsley, mayonnaise and lemon juice in a bowl. Toss lightly to mix. Season with salt and pepper.

Open the pea pods and fill with a generous teaspoon of the crab meat mixture. Arrange close together in a shallow dish and chill until serving time.

You can substitute chopped cooked shrimp or shredded cooked chicken for the crab meat in this recipe if preferred.

Makes 50

Seviche

2 pounds small shrimp
1 cup ketchup
1/2 cup lemon juice
1 small purple onion, slivered

1 medium green bell pepper, slivered
1 tablespoon dried oregano leaves
Tabasco sauce to taste
salt to taste

Cook the shrimp in water to cover in a saucepan just until they turn pink; drain and peel. Combine the ketchup, lemon juice, onion, bell pepper and oregano in a bowl. Season with Tabasco sauce and salt. Add the shrimp and mix well.

Chill the mixture for 12 hours or longer. Serve with salty crackers.

The acid in the lemon juice will "cook" the seafood as it chills. Add 1 part lemon juice to 3 parts ketchup if more sauce is needed.

Serves 8

Olive Bites

2 cups (8 ounces) shredded sharp
   Cheddar cheese
½ cup (1 stick) butter, softened
1½ cups sifted flour
1 teaspoon paprika

¼ teaspoon salt
red pepper to taste
1 (13-ounce) jar pimento-stuffed green
   olives, drained

Combine the cheese and butter in a bowl and mix well. Add the flour, paprika, salt and red pepper and mix to form a dough. Wrap each olive with a portion of the dough, enclosing it completely.

Arrange the olives on an ungreased baking sheet. Bake at 400 degrees for 12 to 15 minutes or until golden brown.

You can prepare the olive bites in advance and freeze until needed. Bake frozen bites for 20 minutes.

Serves 8

SANDESTIN WINE FESTIVAL

The Sandestin Wine Festival has become one of the rites of spring for many people along the Emerald Coast. Hosted each year by Sandestin Golf and Beach Resort, the festival boasts over 500 wines from more than 100 vineyards and includes several charity benefits, a golf tournament, and the Grand Wine Tasting to cap it off. Festival guests are encouraged to sample the wines and ask questions about the vintage. Proceeds benefit the Mattie Kelly Arts Foundation, a nonprofit organization that promotes the arts in the area.

Olive Crostini

1 (8-ounce) loaf French bread
1 (4-ounce) can chopped black
    olives, drained
1/2 cup chopped pimento-stuffed
    green olives
2 garlic cloves, minced
3/4 cup (3 ounces) shredded
    Monterey Jack cheese

1/2 cup (2 ounces) grated
    Parmesan cheese
1/4 cup (1/2 stick) butter or margarine,
    softened
1/4 cup chopped parsley

Cut the bread into 1/4-inch slices. Combine the black olives, green olives, garlic, Monterey Jack cheese, Parmesan cheese, butter and parsley in a bowl; mix well. Spread evenly on the bread slices and arrange on a baking sheet. Broil, leaving the oven door partially open, for 3 to 4 minutes or until the topping is bubbly and golden brown.

Serves 12

Spinach and Feta Crostini

1 (16-ounce) loaf French bread
1 (10-ounce) package frozen chopped
    spinach, thawed and drained
1 small onion, chopped
1 garlic clove, minced
1/2 cup (2 ounces) crumbled feta cheese

1/4 cup mayonnaise
1/4 cup (2 ounces) sour cream
1/4 teaspoon pepper
2 plum tomatoes, thinly sliced
crumbled feta cheese

Cut the bread into 1/2-inch slices. Combine the spinach, onion, garlic, 1/2 cup cheese, mayonnaise, sour cream and pepper in a bowl and mix well. Spread evenly on the bread slices and arrange on a baking sheet. Top each bread slice with a tomato slice. Bake at 350 degrees for 18 minutes or until golden brown. Sprinkle with additional cheese if desired.

Serves 12

The photograph for this recipe appears on page 14.

Spanakopita

2 tablespoons olive oil
2 cups minced onions
2 teaspoons basil
2 teaspoons oregano
1/2 teaspoon salt
2 1/2 pounds fresh spinach leaves,
    finely chopped
5 garlic cloves, minced

3 tablespoons flour
2 1/2 cups (10 ounces) crumbled
    feta cheese
1 cup (8 ounces) cottage cheese
3/4 teaspoon pepper
1 (1-pound) package frozen phyllo
    pastry, thawed
1/3 cup (about) olive oil

Heat 2 tablespoons olive oil in a heavy saucepan over medium heat. Add the onions, basil, oregano and salt. Sauté for 5 minutes or until the onions are tender. Add the spinach and increase the heat to medium-high. Sauté for 6 to 8 minutes or until the spinach is wilted. Stir in the garlic and then the flour. Cook for 2 minutes, stirring constantly. Remove from the heat and stir in the feta cheese, cottage cheese and pepper. Adjust the seasonings.

Remove 1 sheet of phyllo pastry, leaving the remaining sheets covered with a damp towel. Place the pastry in a greased 9×13-inch baking pan, allowing the pastry to extend up the sides of the pan. Brush the pastry lightly with some of the olive oil. Repeat the process until 8 sheets of pastry have been layered and brushed with olive oil. Spread half the spinach mixture in the prepared pan.

Layer 8 additional pastry sheets in the baking pan, brushing each with olive oil. Spread with the remaining spinach mixture. Top with 4 pastry sheets, brushing each with olive oil. Tuck the edges down the sides of the pan. Bake, uncovered, at 375 degrees for 45 minutes or until crisp and golden brown. Cut into squares and serve warm.

Serves 8

GREEK SALSA

Greek Salsa is a great accompaniment to Spanakopita or the Pita Chips on page 32. Combine 1 pound chopped tomatoes with 1/2 cup chopped cucumber, 1/4 cup chopped purple onion, 1 can chopped black olives and 2 tablespoons chopped parsley in a bowl. Whisk 2 tablespoons lemon juice with 1 tablespoon olive oil, 1 or 2 minced garlic cloves, 1/2 teaspoon oregano and 1/8 teaspoon each salt and pepper in a bowl. Add to the tomato mixture and toss to mix well. Sprinkle with 1/2 cup crumbled feta cheese. Chill, covered, for 24 hours before serving.

Crab Island Cheesecake

Phyllo Crust

8 sheets frozen phyllo
    pastry, thawed

melted butter

Filling

2 eggs
16 ounces cream cheese, softened
juice of 1/2 lemon
2 teaspoons Worcestershire sauce
1/4 teaspoon liquid crab boil
1 1/2 teaspoons Old Bay seasoning
1 teaspoon salt
1/8 teaspoon white pepper
1/2 cup chopped onion

1/4 cup chopped green bell pepper
1/4 cup chopped celery
2 tablespoons butter
1 teaspoon crushed garlic
2 green onion tops, finely chopped
2 plum tomatoes, peeled, seeded
    and chopped
8 ounces backfin crab meat
1 teaspoon grated lemon zest

Tartar Sauce Topping

1 cup mayonnaise
1 teaspoon crushed garlic

2 tablespoons minced onion

To *prepare the crust*, remove 1 sheet of the pastry, leaving the remaining sheets covered with a damp towel. Cut the pastry into a 10-inch circle and fit into a 9-inch springform pan, pressing the excess up the side of the pan. Brush lightly with melted butter. Repeat with the remaining pastry sheets. Bake at 325 degrees for 10 minutes.

To *prepare the filling*, combine the eggs and cream cheese in a mixing bowl and beat at high speed until smooth. Add the lemon juice, Worcestershire sauce, crab boil, Old Bay seasoning, salt and white pepper and mix well. Sauté the onion, bell pepper and celery in the butter in a skillet until tender. Add the garlic and green onion tops and sauté lightly. Remove from the heat and stir in the tomatoes and crab meat. Add to the cream cheese mixture and beat until smooth. Stir in the lemon zest. Spoon into the crust in the springform pan. Bake at 325 degrees for 50 minutes or until the top appears dry. Cool on a wire rack. Place on a serving platter and remove the side of the pan.

To *prepare the topping*, combine the mayonnaise, garlic and onion in a bowl and mix well. Spread over the cheesecake.

Serves 12

Mushroom Pâté

1 cup chopped onion
3/4 cup minced scallions
3 ribs celery, chopped
4 garlic cloves, minced
1/2 cup (1 stick) butter
2 pounds mushrooms, sliced
2 cups chopped walnuts or pecans
1 tablespoon dried basil

1 tablespoon dried thyme
1 tablespoon dried oregano
1 1/2 teaspoons dried rosemary
1 1/2 teaspoons salt
pepper to taste
12 ounces cream cheese, cut into pieces
3/4 cup fresh bread crumbs
3 eggs

Sauté the onion, scallions, celery and garlic in the butter in a skillet. Add the mushrooms, walnuts, basil, thyme, oregano, rosemary, salt and pepper and mix well. Cook until the liquid evaporates, stirring frequently. Add the cream cheese, stirring until the cream cheese melts. Process the mixture in a blender or food processor until puréed. Stir in the bread crumbs and eggs.

Spoon the mixture into a greased 5x7-inch loaf pan. Cover with parchment and foil. Bake at 350 degrees for 1 1/2 hours. Remove from the loaf pan to a serving plate and serve warm with sour cream and crackers. You may also cool to room temperature, frost with sour cream and serve chilled. The pâté can also be frozen.

Serves 10 *to* 12

A Taste of 30-A

Northwest Florida's scenic highway 30-A is one of the most beautiful drives in the area, hugging the coast and providing great glimpses of the beaches that keep people coming back in all seasons. Along this route are also some of the best restaurants in the area. A Taste of 30-A, held in the fall, showcases these restaurants and allows locals and visitors alike to sample the local cuisine while strolling along with friends and enjoying cool jazz sounds along the Emerald Coast. Proceeds from the event benefit local charities.

Pineapple Cheese Ball

16 ounces cream cheese, softened
1 (8-ounce) can crushed
   pineapple, drained
1/4 cup chopped green bell pepper
2 tablespoons minced onion

1 tablespoon minced jalapeño chile
Tabasco sauce to taste
1 tablespoon seasoned salt
2 cups chopped pecans

Combine the cream cheese, crushed pineapple, bell pepper, onion, jalapeño chile, Tabasco sauce, seasoned salt and 1 cup of the chopped pecans in a bowl and mix well. Chill in the refrigerator.

Shape into a ball and roll in the remaining 1 cup pecans, coating well. Place on a platter and serve with bite-size crackers.

Serves 12

Fresh Avocado Salsa

1 avocado, chopped
4 plum tomatoes, chopped
1 sweet onion, finely chopped
1 jalapeño chile, seeded and minced

1/4 cup chopped cilantro
3 tablespoons fresh lime juice
2 dashes of pepper sauce
1/2 teaspoon sea salt

Combine the avocado, tomatoes, onion, jalapeño chile and cilantro in a bowl and mix gently. Stir in the lime juice, pepper sauce and sea salt. Chill until serving time. Serve with tortilla chips.

You may also serve over chicken or scrambled eggs.

Serves 6 to 8

Black Bean and Corn Salsa

2 (15-ounce) cans black beans, rinsed
and drained
2 (16-ounce) cans corn, drained
3 medium tomatoes, peeled, seeded
and chopped
2 jalapeño chiles, seeded and
finely chopped

1 cup chopped cilantro
$1/3$ cup lime juice
$1/4$ teaspoon salt
$1/4$ teaspoon pepper
2 avocados, finely chopped

Combine the black beans, corn, tomatoes, jalapeño chiles and cilantro in a bowl and mix gently. Stir in the lime juice, salt and pepper. Chill, covered, until serving time. Add the avocados and mix gently. Serve immediately with tortilla chips.

Serves 12 *to* 14

IS IT RIPE YET?

You can tell that an avocado is ripe when it feels soft but is not mushy when gently squeezed. To speed up the ripening process, wrap the avocado in several pages of newspaper; it will ripen within a day, sometimes within hours.

Key West Mango Salsa

2 cups chopped peeled mango
1 cup chopped red bell pepper
²/₃ cup chopped green onions
¹/₄ cup chopped cilantro
1 jalapeño chile, chopped, or to taste
juice of 1 lime
4 teaspoons olive oil
salt and pepper to taste

Combine the mango, bell pepper, green onions, cilantro and jalapeño chile in a small bowl and mix well. Add the lime juice and olive oil and season with salt and pepper. Chill, covered, in the refrigerator for 1 hour or for up to 3 days. Serve with tortilla chips. You can also serve with fried or grilled fish.

Makes 3 cups

SEEING RED IN SEASIDE

Seaside, Florida, is the site of one of the most anticipated annual wine festivals in the area, the "Seeing Red Wine Festival." Seaside, a small Gulfside town, is an idyllic community that draws locals and visitors year-round and was featured in the movie *The Truman Show* with Jim Carrey. The festival begins with a kick-off dinner at Bud & Alley's Restaurant with a featured winemaker and later includes wine lectures, tastings, and other dinners. This premier wine-tasting event with premium wines and food is a great opportunity to mingle with other wine lovers, but is limited in that only 100 tickets are sold!

Panhandle Caviar

1 (16-ounce) can black-eyed peas,
   rinsed and drained
1 (16-ounce) can corn, rinsed
   and drained
2 medium tomatoes, seeded
   and chopped
1 small red bell pepper, chopped
1 small yellow bell pepper, chopped
1 small green bell pepper, chopped
1 bunch green onions, chopped

$\frac{1}{2}$ cup chopped red onion
$\frac{3}{4}$ cup chopped sweet onion
6 garlic cloves, minced
1 (4-ounce) can chopped black olives
$\frac{1}{2}$ cup chopped cilantro
3 tablespoons lime juice
$\frac{1}{2}$ cup red wine vinegar
1 envelope Italian salad dressing mix
$\frac{1}{2}$ teaspoon salt
$\frac{1}{2}$ teaspoon pepper

Combine the first 12 ingredients in a large bowl. Add the lime juice, vinegar, salad dressing mix, salt and pepper and toss to mix well. Chill, covered, for 8 hours, stirring occasionally. Serve with tortilla chips.

Serves 18 *to* 20

Artichoke Cheese Dip

1 round loaf Hawaiian bread or
   sourdough bread
1 bunch green onions, chopped
6 garlic cloves, minced
2 tablespoons butter
8 ounces cream cheese, chopped

2 cups (16 ounces) sour cream
3 cups (12 ounces) shredded
   Cheddar cheese
$\frac{1}{2}$ teaspoon garlic salt or seasoned salt
1 (10-ounce) can water-pack artichoke
   hearts, drained and cut into quarters

Cut a circle 5 inches in diameter from the top of the bread. Remove the soft bread from the circle and discard; reserve the circle to top the dip. Scoop out the bread from the loaf; reserve the soft bread for another use and the bread shell for the dip. Sauté the green onions and garlic in the butter until wilted. Add the cream cheese, sour cream, Cheddar cheese and garlic salt and mix well. Fold in the artichokes. Spoon into the bread shell and replace the top. Wrap the loaf in a double thickness of heavy-duty foil. Bake at 350 degrees for $1\frac{1}{2}$ hours. Serve warm with French bread slices, crackers, chips or apple slices.

Serves 10

Baba Ghannoujh

1 eggplant
3 garlic cloves, minced
1/2 cup fresh lemon juice
1/2 cup sesame paste (tahini)
1/2 teaspoon salt

1/4 teaspoon black pepper
1/8 teaspoon cayenne pepper
olive oil
minced fresh parsley

Cut the eggplant into halves lengthwise and place cut side down on a greased baking sheet. Bake at 350 degrees for 30 minutes or until very tender. Cool slightly and scoop the pulp into a food processor, discarding the peel. Add the garlic, lemon juice, sesame paste, salt, black pepper and cayenne pepper and process until smooth.

Spoon into a serving dish. Chill, covered, until serving time. Drizzle with olive oil and sprinkle with parsley. Serve with Pita Chips (below), pita bread, crackers or crudités.

Serves 4 to 6

PITA CHIPS

You can't eat too many! These chips are great for hot dips or for Mediterranean appetizers. Cut the edges of four 4-inch pita rounds with kitchen scissors and split into halves horizontally. Combine 1 tablespoon olive oil, 1 tablespoon melted butter, 1/8 teaspoon paprika, 1/8 teaspoon kosher salt and 1/8 teaspoon cayenne pepper in a bowl and mix well. Brush on the rough sides of the pita rounds and cut each round into 6 wedges. Arrange the wedges on a parchment-lined baking sheet and bake at 350 degrees for 8 minutes or until crisp and golden brown.

Hot Pecan Dip

3/4 cup chopped pecans
2 tablespoons butter, melted
1/2 teaspoon salt
8 ounces cream cheese, softened
2 tablespoons milk

1/4 cup finely chopped green bell pepper
1/2 small onion, grated
1/2 teaspoon garlic powder
freshly ground pepper to taste
1/2 cup (4 ounces) sour cream

Combine the pecans, butter and salt in a shallow baking dish and bake at 350 degrees for 15 minutes. Cool for several minutes.

Combine the cream cheese with the milk in a bowl and mix until smooth. Add the bell pepper, onion, garlic powder, pepper and sour cream, mixing well after each addition.

Spoon into an ungreased 8- or 9-inch baking dish. Sprinkle the pecans over the top. Bake at 350 degrees for 20 minutes. Serve hot with crackers.

You may prepare the dip in advance and chill until baking time.

Makes 3 cups

Seaside Shrimp Dip

16 ounces cream cheese, softened
8 ounces whipped cream cheese
1 tablespoon French salad dressing
1 tablespoon Worcestershire sauce
1 tablespoon white vinegar
juice of 1 1/2 to 2 lemons
1 cup (8 ounces) sour cream

2 to 3 teaspoons horseradish
1 teaspoon Tabasco sauce, or to taste
3 tablespoons grated onion
4 garlic cloves, crushed
salt and pepper to taste
2 pounds shrimp, cooked and chopped

Beat the cream cheeses in a mixing bowl until light and fluffy. Add the salad dressing, Worcestershire sauce, vinegar, lemon juice, sour cream, horseradish, Tabasco sauce, onion and garlic. Mix well. Season with salt and pepper. Stir in the shrimp. Chill, covered, for 8 hours or longer before serving.

Serves 12

Refreshing Thai Dip

1 cup (8 ounces) sour cream
¼ cup mayonnaise
2 tablespoons soy sauce
4 green onions with tops, finely chopped

¼ cup chopped parsley
2 tablespoons chopped gingerroot
2 tablespoons chopped cilantro

Combine the sour cream, mayonnaise and soy sauce in a bowl and mix well. Stir in the green onions, parsley, gingerroot and cilantro. Chill, covered, for 1 hour or longer.

Serves 6 to 8

Cocktail Sauce

¼ cup chili sauce
juice of 1 lemon
2 teaspoons Worcestershire sauce

1 teaspoon pepper sauce
1 tablespoon horseradish
2 tablespoons thinly sliced green onions

Combine all the ingredients in a medium bowl and mix well. Store, covered, in the refrigerator for up to 2 weeks. Serve with fresh Gulf shrimp.

Makes 1 cup

The photograph for this recipe appears on page 14.

Crab Meat Butter

1 cup (2 sticks) butter
32 ounces cream cheese

2 pounds lump crab meat, flaked
   and cooked

Melt the butter and cream cheese in a double boiler, stirring to blend well. Fold in the crab meat. Serve in a chafing dish with crackers or chips. You may also spread this on English muffins and top with a poached egg and Hollandaise sauce as a substitute for the Canadian bacon in a coastal version of eggs Benedict.

Makes 8 cups

Coffee Soda

3 cups strong brewed coffee, chilled
1 tablespoon sugar
1 cup half-and-half

4 scoops coffee ice cream
3/4 cup club soda
whipped cream

Mix the first 3 ingredients in a pitcher until smooth. Pour into tall glasses, filling halfway. Add 1 scoop ice cream to each glass and fill with the club soda. Top with whipped cream.

Serves 4

Florida Freeze
Turton Tea

1 cup fresh orange juice
4 teaspoons loose orange tea leaves
2 cups orange sherbet

1/4 cup half-and-half or whole milk
1 orange, sliced

Bring the orange juice to a boil in a small saucepan and stir in the tea leaves. Remove from the heat and steep for 15 minutes. Strain into a blender. Add the sherbet and half-and-half. Process until smooth, pausing at 30-second intervals to stir down the sides. Pour into chilled tall glasses and garnish with orange slices.

Serves 4 to 6

Taste of the Tropics Smoothie

1/2 cup light coconut milk
1/2 cup guava nectar
1/2 cup strawberry sorbet

1 1/2 cups quartered frozen strawberries
1 cup chopped frozen pineapple

Combine the coconut milk, guava nectar and sorbet in a blender and process to mix well. Add the strawberries and pineapple and process until smooth. Pour into glasses.

Serves 2

Olde-Tyme Eggnog

12 egg yolks
1½ cups superfine sugar
4 cups whole milk
4 cups heavy cream
4 cups bourbon
¼ cup dark rum

1½ cups Cognac
¼ teaspoon cinnamon
12 egg whites
2 cups heavy cream
freshly grated nutmeg

Beat the egg yolks in a mixing bowl until light yellow and thick. Add the sugar gradually, beating until the sugar dissolves. Whisk in the milk and 4 cups cream. Add the bourbon, rum, Cognac and cinnamon, whisking constantly until smooth. Chill until serving time.

Beat the egg whites in a mixing bowl until stiff peaks form. Fold into the egg yolk mixture. Beat 2 cups cream in a mixing bowl until soft peaks form. Fold into the eggnog. Pour into a punch bowl and sprinkle with nutmeg.

To avoid the possibility of salmonella from uncooked eggs, you can use an equivalent amount of egg substitute.

Serves 16

Bloody Marys for a Crowd

1 (48-ounce) can tomato juice
1 (48-ounce) can vegetable
    juice cocktail
¼ cup lemon juice
¼ cup Worcestershire sauce

Tabasco sauce to taste
2 teaspoons horseradish
2 cups premium vodka
celery sticks
lemon wedges

Combine the tomato juice, vegetable juice cocktail, lemon juice, Worcestershire sauce, Tabasco sauce and horseradish in a 1-gallon pitcher and mix well. Stir in the vodka. Chill in the refrigerator. Pour into glasses and garnish with celery sticks and lemon wedges.

Serves 16

Chocolate Royale Martini

3 tablespoons chocolate liqueur
1 tablespoon sweetened cocoa powder

1 chocolate kiss
1/4 cup premium vodka

Moisten the rim of a chilled martini glass with a small amount of the liqueur; dip into the cocoa powder to coat the rim. Place the chocolate kiss in the glass. Shake the vodka and the remaining liqueur with ice in a shaker. Strain into the glass.

For a White Chocolate Martini, use confectioners' sugar instead of cocoa powder, a white chocolate truffle and a white chocolate liqueur.

Serves 1

Grateful Grapefruit Blush

3/4 cup sugar
2 cups water
1 cup grapefruit juice
3 tablespoons lemon juice

1/2 cup chopped grapefruit sections
2 cups sparkling mineral water, chilled
1 1/2 cups vodka

Combine the sugar and water in a small saucepan and bring to a boil, stirring constantly to dissolve the sugar. Remove from the heat and cool.

Combine the sugar syrup with the grapefruit juice, lemon juice and chopped grapefruit in a pitcher; mix well. Chill, covered, for 2 hours or longer. Stir in the mineral water and vodka at serving time.

Serves 8

Infused Pineapple Vodka
Café Thirty-A

1 medium ripe pineapple, peeled　　　　**1 liter Skyy or Absolut vodka**

Cut the pineapple into 1-inch cubes. Place in an airtight jar. Add the vodka, reserving the empty vodka bottle; seal the jar. Let stand for 1 week. Strain the mixture into a pitcher, reserving the pineapple and the vodka. Squeeze the juice from the pineapple into the pitcher. Place a funnel in the reserved vodka bottle and line it with a coffee filter. Pour the vodka into the bottle. Store in the refrigerator for up to 1 month. Serve over ice.

Makes 1 liter

Infused Cranberry Vodka

5 cups cranberries　　　　　　　　　　**1 1/4 cups sugar**
2 1/4 cups water　　　　　　　　　　　**2 cups vodka**

Combine the cranberries, water and sugar in a heavy saucepan and bring to a boil, stirring to dissolve the sugar. Remove from the heat and cool. Stir in the vodka, reserving the empty bottle. Let stand, covered, at room temperature for 2 days. Place a funnel in the reserved vodka bottle and line it with a coffee filter. Pour the vodka into the bottle. Store in the refrigerator for up to 1 month. Serve over ice, with or without tonic.

Makes 4 1/2 cups

EMERALD EVENING

An Emerald Evening by the Coast, held each spring, is one of the signature fund-raising and social events of the Junior League of the Emerald Coast. The benefit raises funds for the many community service projects the League participates in. For the last two years the event has benefited the restoration of the historic Gulfview Hotel in Old Camp Walton. The gala event, generally featured in *The Emerald Coast Magazine*, includes coastal cuisine, live entertainment, and both silent and live auctions. Grab a friend, get ready to bid, and look forward to a great time with the ladies of the League.

Grapefruit Margaritas

1 1/2 cups grapefruit juice
juice of 1 lime
3/4 cup tequila

1/3 cup Grand Marnier
1/3 cup sugar
lime slices

Combine the grapefruit juice, lime juice, tequila, Grand Marnier and sugar in a blender. Fill with chipped ice and blend at high speed until smooth. Pour into glasses and garnish with lime slices.

Serves 3 or 4

Festive Mimosas

1/4 cup Grand Marnier
2 tablespoons sugar
1 bottle Champagne

1 cup fresh orange juice
1/4 cup Grand Marnier

Pour 1/4 cup Grand Marnier into a shallow dish and place the sugar in a saucer. Dip the rims of Champagne glasses into the Grand Marnier and then into the sugar to coat the rims. Combine the Champagne with the orange juice and 1/4 cup Grand Marnier in a pitcher and mix gently. Serve immediately in the prepared glasses.

Serves 6

The photograph for this recipe appears on page 46.

Cosmopolitan

½ cup Infused Vodka (page 38)
2 tablespoons Triple Sec, Cointreau or
   Grand Marnier

splash of cranberry juice
lime wedge

Combine the vodka, Triple Sec and cranberry juice in a glass and mix gently. Garnish with a lime wedge.

Serves 1

Spiced Wine

2 teaspoons whole allspice
2 (2-inch) cinnamon sticks
10 whole cloves

4 bottles burgundy
½ cup sugar
½ teaspoon angostura bitters

Tie the allspice, cinnamon and cloves in a cheesecloth bag and combine with the wine in a large saucepan. Stir in the sugar and bitters. Heat just until the sugar dissolves, stirring constantly; do not boil. Keep hot until serving time. Discard the spice bag and serve from a heated punch bowl.

Serves 32

HOW TO HOST A WINE TASTING

Don't feel that you know enough to host a blind wine tasting? It really is very easy. Just ask each guest to bring a bottle of either chardonnay or cabernet in a brown paper sack. You may want to ask couples to bring one inexpensive wine and one moderately priced one. Leave the wine in the bags, tying them closed with decorative ribbons. Have guests taste the wines during cocktails and score them with a rating scale. Suggestions for a rating scale include:

10 points - Ooh, I feel like I'm in Napa Valley.
 8 points - This tastes like more than I can afford.
 6 points - This must be something I can afford.
 4 points - Screw top, right?
 2 points - Grape juice with a kick.

Garden Sangria

1 gallon dry white wine
2 cups brandy
1 cup orange liqueur
4 oranges, thinly sliced

1 liter club soda or ginger ale, chilled
1 quart whole strawberries
2 lemons and 2 limes, thinly sliced
1 cup red seedless grapes

Combine the wine, brandy, orange liqueur and oranges in a large container. Chill, covered, for 8 hours. Combine with the club soda, strawberries, lemons, limes and grapes in a punch bowl; mix gently. Serve over ice and garnish with additional slices of lemon, lime and orange.

Makes 1½ gallons

White Sangria

2 (750 milliliter) bottles sauvignon blanc
1 cup brandy
1½ cups sugar
2 lemons and 2 limes, thinly sliced

1 Red Delicious apple, thinly sliced
2 (1 liter) bottles lemon-lime sparkling
   water, chilled
1 cup frozen green grapes

Combine the wine, brandy and sugar in a large pitcher and mix gently to dissolve the sugar. Add the sliced lemons, limes and apple. Chill for 2 hours or longer. Add the sparkling water and grapes and mix gently. Serve over ice.

Makes 9 cups

Sustainer Punch

3 bottles sauterne
2 cups sugar
2 cups brandy, chilled

6 bottles Champagne
ginger ale
frozen grape clusters

Combine the sauterne and sugar in a punch bowl and stir gently to dissolve the sugar. Stir in the brandy and Champagne. Add enough ginger ale to dilute the punch to taste and mix gently. Ladle over frozen grape clusters in punch cups to serve.

Serves 30

Oh My, Junior League Punch

Frozen Decorative Ring

1 orange, sliced
1 lemon, sliced

1 lime, sliced
4 cups cranberry juice

Punch

1 (6-ounce) can frozen orange juice
  concentrate, thawed
1 (12-ounce) can frozen lemonade
  concentrate, thawed

³/₄ cup pineapple juice
2 liters lemon-lime soda
3 cups white wine
3 cups Champagne

To *prepare the ring*, arrange the orange slices, lemon slices and lime slices in a mold and add the cranberry juice. Freeze until firm.

To *prepare the punch*, combine the orange juice concentrate, lemonade concentrate, pineapple juice, lemon-lime soda, white wine and Champagne in a punch bowl and mix gently. Unmold the decorative ring and float it in the punch.

Serves 32

BEAUTY ON ICE

Floral or fruited ice cubes and molds are a good way to keep your punch cold and add some unexpected beauty as well. Fill ice cube trays with the punch or one of the fruit juices in the punch if the punch is alcoholic, since the alcohol would keep the cubes from freezing. Place an edible flower or appropriate small fruit, such as a raspberry, blueberry or grape, in each cube compartment. Cover with plastic wrap and freeze until firm. Float in the punch bowl or use in individual glasses.

Destin Boat Punch

2 (46-ounce) cans pineapple juice
1 (half-gallon) container orange juice
   and tangerine juice blend
1 (half-gallon) container tropical fruit
   juice blend
1 cup light rum
1 cup dark rum

3 cups coconut-flavored rum
3 cups mandarin-flavored vodka
1 (16-ounce) can pineapple chunks,
   drained
1 (13-ounce) jar maraschino cherries
1 orange, thinly sliced
1 lime, thinly sliced

Combine the pineapple juice and mixed fruit juices in a 5-gallon container. Add the rums and vodka and mix gently. Stir in the pineapple, undrained cherries, orange slices and lime slices. Chill until serving time.

Serves 48

Pirate Punch

2 to 3 (1.75-liter) bottles light rum
1 (1.75-liter) bottle Captain Morgan's
   Parrot Bay coconut-flavored rum

9 (46-ounce) cans pineapple juice
1 (46-ounce) can Hawaiian Punch

Combine the rums in a 5-gallon container. Add the pineapple juice and punch and mix well. Serve over ice. This recipe can be reduced to serve a smaller gathering.

Serves 30

FORT WALTON'S FAVORITE PIRATE

He's not as famous as Bluebeard or Captain Morgan, but Billy Bowlegs has invaded the Fort Walton Beach area for more than forty years. The original Billy Bowlegs was actually buccaneer William Augustus Bowles, who came to the area in 1799. The Billy Bowlegs Festival is held each year in late spring and is highlighted by the "invasion" of Captain Billy with his queen and crew at Fort Walton Beach Landing. Each year a mock battle ensues, and the pirates defeat the city's militia. The festival is filled with fun and activities for all ages, including arts and crafts, treasure hunts, amusement rides, and great food. Grab an eye patch and a bandanna and join in the fun!

Coffees of the World

Irish Coffee
3/4 cup hot brewed coffee
3 tablespoons Irish whiskey

1 tablespoon Bailey's Irish cream
whipped cream

Italian Coffee
3/4 cup strong hot brewed coffee
1 1/2 tablespoons brandy

1 1/2 tablespoons amaretto
whipped cream

Jamaican Coffee
3/4 cup hot brewed coffee
2 tablespoons Jamaican rum

2 tablespoons Tía Maria
whipped cream and ground allspice

Mexican Coffee
3/4 cup hot brewed coffee
2 tablespoons Kahlúa

1 tablespoons tequila
whipped cream

For *Irish Coffee*, combine the coffee with the Irish whiskey and Bailey's Irish cream in a cup. Stir to mix and top with whipped cream.

For *Italian Coffee*, combine the coffee with the brandy and amaretto in a cup. Stir to mix and top with whipped cream.

For *Jamaican Coffee*, combine the coffee with the rum and Tía Maria in a cup. Stir to mix and top with whipped cream and a sprinkle of allspice.

For *Mexican Coffee*, combine the coffee with the Kahlúa and tequila in a cup. Stir to mix and top with whipped cream.

Each serves 1

Praline Coffee

3 cups hot brewed coffee
²/₃ to ¾ cup packed light brown sugar
¾ cup half-and-half

¾ cup praline liqueur or any nut-flavor
  liqueur
sweetened whipped cream

Combine the coffee with the brown sugar and half-and-half in a large saucepan. Heat over medium heat, stirring constantly; do not boil. Stir in the liqueur and pour into cups. Top with sweetened whipped cream.

Serves 5

Honey Citrus Tea

grated zest and juice of 8 oranges
grated zest and juice of 6 lemons
2 gallons water

16 tea bags
2 (2-inch) cinnamon sticks
1 cup honey

Combine the orange zest, orange juice, lemon zest, lemon juice, water, tea bags and cinnamon in a large saucepan. Bring to a boil over medium-high heat and remove from the heat. Steep for 15 minutes. Strain, discarding the tea bags and cinnamon. Combine with the honey in the saucepan and heat to the desired serving temperature.

Serves 20

Crab Meat Eggs Benedict

1/4 cup (1/2 stick) unsalted butter
2 shallots, minced
2 tablespoons Cognac
2 1/4 cups heavy cream
grated zest of 1 lemon
1 teaspoon chopped fresh tarragon

salt and freshly ground pepper to taste
4 English muffins, split
8 teaspoons unsalted butter, softened
8 eggs
2 cups jumbo lump crab meat, rinsed
1 teaspoon chopped fresh chives

Melt 1/4 cup butter in a medium skillet. Add the shallots and sauté until translucent. Add the Cognac and cook for 3 minutes or until most of the liquid has evaporated. Add the cream and cook for 7 minutes or until thickened and reduced by half. Strain into a double boiler. Add the lemon zest, tarragon, salt and pepper. Keep warm over warm water.

Spread each muffin half with 1 teaspoon of the butter and arrange on a baking sheet. Toast in the oven until light brown. Turn off the oven. Cover the muffins with foil and let stand in the oven to keep warm.

Bring 1/2 inch of water to a simmer in a deep skillet. Break each egg into a small dish and slide gently into the water 1 at a time, holding the dish just above the surface of the water. Poach for 3 to 5 minutes or until done to taste, turning gently. Remove carefully to a warmed paper towel-lined plate with a slotted spoon.

Flake the crab meat and add to the sauce in the double boiler and cook until heated through. Place 2 muffin halves on each plate. Remove the crab meat from the sauce with a slotted spoon and place on the muffins. Top each with 1 egg and some of the sauce. Sprinkle with the chives and serve immediately.

Serves 4

MAKE-AHEAD EGGS BENEDICT

Arrange 6 buttered English muffin halves in a buttered baking dish. Top each muffin half with a slice of Canadian bacon. Combine 12 eggs with 1/2 cup milk and 1/2 cup shredded Cheddar cheese in a bowl and mix well. Scramble in a buttered nonstick skillet until soft-set. Spoon over the muffins. Prepare Hollandaise sauce from a packaged mix; the stabilizers added to commercial mixes make the sauce more forgiving than homemade for make-ahead purposes. Chill, covered, until baking time. Bake, covered, at 350 degrees for 20 minutes or until hot.

The photograph for this recipe appears on page 46.

Deviled Egg Bake

6 hard-cooked eggs, cut into halves
3 tablespoons mayonnaise
1/2 teaspoon prepared mustard
salt and pepper to taste
3 to 4 tablespoons margarine
1/3 cup flour
1/3 cup milk
Worcestershire sauce to taste

1 teaspoon salt
seasoning blend to taste
1 3/4 cups (7 ounces) shredded
    Cheddar cheese
1 (4-ounce) can sliced black olives
3/4 cup fresh bread crumbs (optional)
2 to 3 tablespoons melted butter or
    margarine (optional)

Scoop the egg yolks into a bowl, reserving the whites. Mash the yolks and add the mayonnaise and mustard; mix until smooth. Season with salt and pepper to taste. Spoon into the reserved egg whites and arrange in a baking dish.

Melt the margarine in a medium saucepan. Add the flour and cook until bubbly. Add the milk, Worcestershire sauce and 1 teaspoon salt. Add seasoning blend and pepper to taste. Whisk until smooth and cook until thickened, whisking constantly. Spoon over the eggs.

Sprinkle with the cheese and olives. Top with the bread crumbs and drizzle with the melted butter. Bake, uncovered, at 350 degrees for 25 minutes or until bubbly and golden brown.

Serves 6

Baked Eggs with Blue Crab

10 eggs
1/3 cup milk
8 ounces cream cheese, cubed
6 ounces lump crab meat

1/2 teaspoon salt
1/4 teaspoon freshly ground pepper
1/4 cup (1/2 stick) butter
1 1/2 tablespoons chopped fresh dill weed

Whisk the eggs with the milk in a large bowl until light and fluffy. Fold in the cream cheese and crab meat. Season with the salt and pepper. Melt the butter in a baking dish and swirl to coat the dish well. Spoon the egg mixture into the prepared dish. Sprinkle with the dill weed. Bake at 350 degrees for 30 minutes. Serve hot.

Serves 8

Spinach and Prosciutto Frittata

5 eggs
2/3 cup milk
salt and pepper to taste

4 ounces prosciutto, sliced into strips
1 1/2 cups thinly sliced spinach leaves
1/3 cup crumbled goat cheese

Whisk the eggs with the milk in a bowl until smooth. Season with salt and pepper. Add the prosciutto and spinach and mix well. Pour into a nonstick ovenproof skillet. Cook over medium heat until nearly set, lifting the edges to let uncooked portions come into contact with the skillet.

Remove from the heat and top with the cheese. Broil until the eggs are set and the cheese is golden brown.

Serves 4

Herbed Brie Omelet

1 ounce Brie cheese
2 tablespoons chopped flat-leaf parsley
3 eggs

2 tablespoons clarified butter
salt and freshly ground pepper to taste

Cut the rind from the Brie cheese and roll the cheese in the parsley. Beat the eggs in a bowl until combined but not frothy. Heat an omelet pan over high heat and add the clarified butter. Heat until very hot but not smoking. Pour the eggs into the skillet. Cook until nearly set, using a spatula to stir the eggs from the edge of the pan and shaking the pan gently to prevent sticking; turn down the heat if necessary.

Place the cheese in the center of the omelet just before the eggs are set. Season with salt and pepper. Fold over the omelet to enclose the cheese and remove to a serving plate. Serve immediately.

Serves 1 to 2

Mexicali Quiche with Avocado Topping

Avocado Topping

2 avocados
1 tomato, peeled, seeded and chopped
3 green onions with tops, chopped
2 to 3 tablespoons lime juice

3 dashes of Tabasco sauce
1 teaspoon garlic powder
salt to taste

Quiche

6 (6-inch) corn tortillas
8 ounces hot bulk pork sausage
1/2 cup finely chopped white onion
1 1/2 tablespoons taco seasoning
3 eggs, lightly beaten
1 (4-ounce) can chopped green chiles

1 1/2 cups half-and-half
1/2 teaspoon salt
pepper to taste
1 1/2 cups (6 ounces) shredded
    Monterey Jack cheese

To *prepare the topping*, mash the avocados in a bowl. Add the tomato, green onions, lime juice, Tabasco sauce, garlic powder and salt and mix well. Chill until serving time.

To *prepare the quiche*, bring 2 inches of water to a boil in a large skillet. Dip each tortilla into the water to soften and drain on paper towels. Arrange in a greased quiche pan or pie plate.

Cook the sausage with the onion and taco seasoning in a skillet over medium heat, stirring until the sausage is brown and crumbly; drain. Combine the eggs, half the green chiles, the half-and-half, salt and pepper in a large bowl and mix well. Add the sausage.

Spread half the sausage mixture over the tortillas. Sprinkle with half the cheese and the remaining sausage mixture. Bake at 350 degrees for 20 minutes. Sprinkle with the remaining cheese and bake for 5 minutes longer. Let stand for several minutes. Sprinkle with the remaining green chiles and serve with the avocado topping.

Serves 6

Mushroom and Swiss Cheese Quiche

1 teaspoon butter
1¼ cups chopped onions
2 cups sliced mushrooms
½ teaspoon dry mustard
⅛ teaspoon thyme
½ teaspoon salt
¼ teaspoon pepper

4 eggs
1½ cups milk
2 tablespoons flour
1¾ cups (7 ounces) shredded
    Swiss cheese
1 unbaked (10-inch) pie shell
paprika to taste

Melt the butter in a small skillet over medium heat. Add the onions and sauté for 2 to 3 minutes or until tender. Add the mushrooms, dry mustard, thyme, salt and pepper. Sauté for 5 minutes longer. Remove from the heat.

Combine the eggs, milk and flour in a blender or food processor and process until smooth.

Sprinkle the cheese in the pie shell and spread the mushroom mixture over the cheese. Pour the egg mixture over the top and sprinkle with paprika. Bake at 375 degrees for 40 minutes or until the center is set. Serve hot or at room temperature.

Serves 6

CRAB ISLAND

The Emerald Coast has more than twenty-four miles of powdery white beaches. The extremely soft white sand is sculpted from Appalachian quartz and helps to contribute to the beautiful hues of blue and emerald-green waters. One of the most popular and noteworthy sandbars in the area is locally referred to as Crab Island. It can be seen from the Destin bridge. During any given spring or summer weekend, countless boats drop anchor there to allow their passengers to frolic in the shallow surf.

Life in Paradise Scrambled Eggs

8 eggs
3 tablespoons heavy cream
2 tablespoons sour cream
salt and freshly ground pepper to taste

2 tablespoons butter
1/2 cup (2 ounces) shredded
   Cheddar cheese

Combine the eggs, cream, sour cream, salt and pepper in a bowl and beat until fluffy. Melt the butter in a nonstick skillet. Add the egg mixture and cook over medium heat until nearly set, stirring frequently. Add the cheese and cook until done to taste, stirring frequently.

Serves 4

Sausage Grits

1 cup quick-cooking grits
4 cups water
2 tablespoons butter
1 pound mild or hot bulk pork
   sausage, crumbled
1 garlic clove, minced
1 teaspoon hot sauce

3/4 teaspoon pepper
2 eggs
2 cups (8 ounces) shredded sharp
   Cheddar cheese
1 (7-ounce) can chopped green chiles
1/2 cup chopped red bell pepper

Combine the grits and water in a 3-quart saucepan and bring to a boil over high heat, stirring to mix well. Add the butter and reduce the heat to low. Cook, covered, for 5 minutes or until the grits are tender, stirring frequently. Cool for 30 minutes.

Brown the sausage in a skillet, stirring until crumbly; drain. Stir in the garlic, hot sauce and pepper. Beat the eggs in a large bowl. Add the sausage mixture, cheese, green chiles and bell pepper and mix well. Stir in the grits.

Spoon into a buttered 9×13-inch baking dish. Bake, uncovered, at 350 degrees for 45 minutes. Let stand for 5 minutes. Cut into squares to serve.

Serves 8 to 10

Sherried Cheese Grits

8 cups water
1 teaspoon salt
2 cups quick-cooking grits
1 roll garlic cheese
1 cup (2 sticks) butter
2 garlic cloves, minced

2 tablespoons sherry
2 tablespoons Worcestershire sauce
Tabasco sauce to taste
pepper to taste
2 eggs

Bring the water and salt to a boil in a large saucepan. Add the grits gradually, stirring constantly. Cook for 2 1/2 minutes, stirring frequently. Add the cheese, butter, garlic, sherry, Worcestershire sauce, Tabasco sauce and pepper; mix well. Let stand until cool.

Beat the eggs in a bowl. Add to the grits mixture and mix well. Spoon into a buttered baking dish. Bake at 400 degrees for 1 hour. Serve hot.

Serves 12

Apple Oatmeal Breakfast Pudding

2 cups milk
2 tablespoons brown sugar
1 tablespoon butter
1/4 teaspoon cinnamon
1/4 teaspoon salt

1 cup rolled oats
1 cup chopped peeled apple
1/2 cup raisins
1 tablespoon brown sugar

Combine the milk, 2 tablespoons brown sugar, the butter, cinnamon and salt in a saucepan. Bring just to a simmer. Stir in the oats, apple and raisins. Cook just until bubbles appear at the edge of the saucepan.

Spoon into a lightly buttered 1 1/2-quart baking dish. Bake at 350 degrees for 15 minutes. Sprinkle 1 tablespoon brown sugar over the top and bake for 15 minutes longer. Serve with cream or half-and-half.

Serves 4

Broiled Grapefruit

2 large grapefruit, chilled
¾ cup packed light brown sugar
3 tablespoons unsalted butter, melted

1 teaspoon cinnamon
½ teaspoon nutmeg

Cut the grapefruit into halves crosswise; cut a thin slice off the bottoms of the halves to enable them to stand upright. Cut around the sections with a serrated knife. Arrange in a baking dish.

Combine the brown sugar, butter, cinnamon and nutmeg in a small bowl and mix well. Sprinkle over the grapefruit. Broil for 2 to 3 minutes or until the topping is bubbly and caramelized. Remove to serving dishes and serve immediately.

Serves 4

Sparkling Grapefruit

2 large pink or ruby red grapefruit
¼ cup sugar

¼ cup Campari
pomegranate seeds (optional)

Peel the grapefruit and remove the sections, discarding the membranes. Combine the sugar and Campari in a large bowl and mix well. Add the grapefruit sections and mix gently to coat well. Chill for 1 hour or longer. Spoon into serving dishes and sprinkle with pomegranate seeds.

Serves 4

The photograph for this recipe appears on page 46.

Amaretto French Toast

6 (1-inch) slices French bread
4 eggs
1/2 cup milk
1 tablespoon dark brown sugar
2 tablespoons amaretto
1 teaspoon almond extract

1/2 teaspoon nutmeg
3 tablespoons butter
1/4 cup sliced almonds, lightly toasted
confectioners' sugar
warm maple syrup

Arrange the bread slices in a 9×13-inch baking dish. Combine the eggs, milk, brown sugar, amaretto, almond extract and nutmeg in a bowl and whisk until smooth. Pour over the bread slices and let stand for 5 minutes, turning once. Chill, covered, in the refrigerator for 8 hours.

Place the butter in a 10×15-inch baking pan. Melt in a 400-degree oven. Arrange the bread slices in the prepared baking pan. Bake for 15 minutes. Turn the slices over and bake for 8 to 10 minutes longer or until golden brown. Sprinkle with the almonds and dust with confectioners' sugar. Top with warm maple syrup.

Serves 6

Hot Buttered Rum Pancakes

1 1/3 cups flour
2 tablespoons sugar
1 tablespoon baking powder
1/4 teaspoon ground cloves
salt to taste
2 eggs

1 cup milk
1/4 cup (1/2 stick) butter, melted
   and cooled
1 tablespoon dark rum, or 1 teaspoon
   rum extract
1 teaspoon vanilla extract

Combine the flour, sugar, baking powder, cloves and salt in a large bowl and mix well. Beat the eggs in a medium bowl. Add the milk, butter, rum and vanilla to the eggs; whisk to blend well. Add to the flour mixture and mix just until smooth. Ladle onto an oiled medium-hot griddle. Cook until bubbles appear and begin to pop. Turn and cook for 1 to 2 minutes longer or until golden brown. Serve with additional melted butter.

You may add 1/2 cup semisweet chocolate chips if desired and serve with whipped cream.

Serves 3 or 4

Sour Cherry Scones

1¼ cups whole wheat flour
2 cups all-purpose flour
¾ cup sugar
2½ teaspoons baking powder
1 teaspoon baking soda
½ teaspoon salt
2¼ cups rolled oats
1½ cups coarsely chopped fresh
    sour cherries
1 cup plus 2 tablespoons (2¼ sticks)
    unsalted butter, chilled and
    cut into ½-inch pieces
⅔ cup buttermilk
1½ tablespoons heavy cream
1 to 2 tablespoons sugar

Combine the whole wheat flour, all-purpose flour, ¾ cup sugar, the baking powder, baking soda, salt and oats in a large mixing bowl. Add the cherries and mix well. Add the butter and mix at medium speed until the mixture resembles coarse crumbs. Add the buttermilk and mix just until the buttermilk is incorporated.

Pat into a 4×15-inch rectangle on a lightly floured surface. Score into 10 triangles. Freeze, covered, for 2 hours or for up to 3 weeks. Remove from the freezer and cut into triangles along the score lines with a sharp knife.

Arrange the triangles 2 inches apart on a parchment-lined baking sheet. Brush with the cream and sprinkle with 1 to 2 tablespoons sugar. Bake at 350 degrees for 30 minutes or until golden brown. Serve warm.

You can substitute dried cherries, dried cranberries or fresh blueberries for the cherries when they are out of season.

Makes 10

Gingerbread Waffles

1 cup molasses	2 cups flour
½ cup (1 stick) butter	1 ½ teaspoons ginger
½ cup buttermilk	½ teaspoon cinnamon
1 egg	¼ teaspoon ground cloves
1 ½ teaspoons baking soda	½ teaspoon salt

Combine the molasses and butter in a saucepan and heat until the butter melts, stirring to blend well; do not boil. Cool slightly and add the buttermilk, egg and baking soda; mix well.

Sift the flour, ginger, cinnamon, cloves and salt into a large bowl. Add the molasses mixture and mix until smooth.

Ladle onto a heated greased waffle iron and cook until golden brown using the manufacturer's directions. Serve with Ginger Syrup (below), additional molasses or chocolate sauce.

Serves 6

Ginger Syrup

1 (1-inch) piece gingerroot	1 whole clove
1 cup sugar	1 teaspoon grated lemon zest
1 cup water	

Cut the unpeeled gingerroot into thin slices. Combine the slices with the sugar, water, clove and lemon zest in a saucepan. Bring to a boil over high heat. Reduce the heat to medium and cook for 5 to 6 minutes or until syrupy, stirring constantly.

Cool the mixture for 15 minutes. Strain into a small pitcher. Serve with Gingerbread Waffles (above), pancakes or oatmeal.

Makes 1 cup

Blueberry French Toast Bake

Blueberry French Toast

9 cups French bread cubes

8 ounces cream cheese, cubed

8 ounces fresh or thawed
   frozen blueberries

2 cups milk

6 eggs

1 teaspoon vanilla extract

¼ cup (½ stick) butter, melted

⅓ cup maple-flavored syrup

cinnamon to taste

Brown Sugar Syrup

1 cup packed brown sugar

1 cup heavy cream

1 cup light corn syrup

salt to taste

To *prepare the French toast*, sprinkle half the bread cubes in a greased 2-quart baking dish. Add the cream cheese cubes and blueberries. Top with the remaining bread cubes.

Combine the milk, eggs and vanilla in a bowl and mix well. Pour over the layers in the baking dish and press down lightly to saturate the bread with the liquid. Combine the butter and syrup in a bowl and mix well. Pour over the layers and sprinkle lightly with cinnamon.

Chill the mixture, covered, for 2 hours or longer. Bake at 325 degrees for 30 to 40 minutes or until golden brown and set.

To *prepare the syrup*, combine the brown sugar, cream, corn syrup and salt in a small saucepan. Cook over low heat until smooth, stirring to blend well; do not boil. Serve with the French toast.

You may microwave the syrup if preferred.

Serves 10

Cinnamon Roll Bundt Cake

24 frozen yeast rolls
1 cup packed brown sugar
¼ cup sugar
1 (4-ounce) package butterscotch
   cook-and-serve pudding mix

1 teaspoon cinnamon
1 cup chopped pecans
¾ cup (1½ sticks) butter, melted

Arrange the frozen rolls in a greased bundt pan. Combine the brown sugar, sugar, pudding mix, cinnamon and pecans in a bowl and mix well. Sprinkle over the rolls. Drizzle with the melted butter. Place in an unheated oven and let rise for 8 hours.

Remove the rolls from the oven and preheat it to 350 degrees. Bake the rolls for 30 to 35 minutes or until golden brown. Let stand for 10 minutes, then invert onto a large serving platter. Serve immediately.

Serves 6 to 8

THE HISTORIC GULFVIEW HOTEL

The historic Gulfview Hotel was constructed by L.I. Smith in 1906 as a hunting and fishing lodge. In 1913, Theo Staff visited and decided it was a perfect place to raise a family, so he purchased the hotel and operated it until 1986. In its heyday, the hotel served as a social community center and today is the only remaining structure in Ft. Walton Beach that represents the city's early years as a resort. The hotel was listed on the National Register of Historic Places in 1992. The structure had deteriorated significantly, however, between 1986 and 1998, and the owners were financially unable to renovate it. In 1998, the granddaughters of Theo Staff purchased the structure and donated it to the Junior League. Since that time, the League has worked hard toward the renovations and preservation, which are finally complete. The Gulfview Hotel will be added to the Historic Walking Tour and is open to the public for touring.

Raspberry Yogurt Coffee Cake

2 cups sifted flour
1/2 teaspoon baking powder
1 teaspoon baking soda
1/4 teaspoon salt
1/2 cup (1 stick) butter or
    margarine, softened

1 cup packed brown sugar
1 egg
1 teaspoon vanilla extract
1 cup raspberry yogurt
raspberry jam
confectioners' sugar

Sift the flour, baking powder, baking soda and salt together. Cream the butter and brown sugar in a mixing bowl until light and fluffy. Beat in the egg and vanilla. Add the flour mixture alternately with the yogurt, mixing well after each addition.

    Spoon half the batter into a greased bundt pan. Dot with tablespoons of raspberry jam and swirl lightly to mix. Top with the remaining batter. Bake at 350 degrees for 30 minutes. Invert the coffee cake onto a serving platter and sprinkle with confectioners' sugar. Serve warm or cooled.

Serves 12

Blueberry Muffins

1 cup blueberries
1 1/2 cups flour
1 teaspoon baking powder
1/2 teaspoon salt
1/2 cup shortening

1 cup sugar
2 egg yolks, beaten
2 egg whites
1 teaspoon vanilla extract
sugar

Toss the blueberries with a small amount of the flour in a bowl, coating well. Sift the remaining flour with the baking powder and salt 3 times. Combine the shortening, 1 cup sugar and the egg yolks in a mixing bowl and beat until light and smooth. Add the flour mixture and mix well.

    Beat the egg whites in a mixing bowl until stiff peaks form. Fold into the batter with the vanilla and blueberries. Spoon into greased muffin cups. Bake at 350 degrees for 20 to 25 minutes or until golden brown. Sprinkle with additional sugar while still warm.

Makes 1 dozen

Doughnut Muffins

6 cups flour
5 teaspoons baking powder
½ teaspoon baking soda
1 teaspoon nutmeg
1¾ teaspoons salt
1⅔ cups milk
¼ cup buttermilk
1½ cups (3 sticks) unsalted
   butter, softened

1¾ cups sugar
4 eggs
2 tablespoons cinnamon
2 cups sugar
1 cup (2 sticks) unsalted butter, melted,
   or more as needed

Sift the flour, baking powder, baking soda, nutmeg and salt together. Mix the milk and buttermilk in a bowl. Cream 1½ cups butter and 1¾ cups sugar in a mixing bowl until light and fluffy. Beat in the eggs 1 at a time.

Add ¼ of the sifted dry ingredients to the batter and mix well. Add the milk mixture and the remaining dry ingredients alternately ⅓ at a time, mixing just until smooth after each addition.

Spoon the batter into greased and floured muffin cups, filling even with the tops of the cups. Bake at 350 degrees for 30 to 35 minutes or until the muffins are firm to the touch. Remove to a wire rack and cool completely.

Mix the cinnamon and 2 cups sugar in a bowl. Brush the muffins all over with the melted butter or dip completely into the melted butter. Roll in the cinnamon-sugar mixture, coating evenly.

Makes 2 dozen

Cranberry Muffins

3/4 cup whole wheat flour
3/4 cup all-purpose flour
1 1/2 cups packed brown sugar
2 teaspoons baking powder
1 teaspoon baking soda
1 1/2 teaspoons cinnamon

1/8 teaspoon salt
1 egg
3/4 cup buttermilk
2 tablespoons vegetable oil
3/4 cup sweetened dried cranberries
2 tablespoons brown sugar

Mix the whole wheat flour, all-purpose flour, 1 1/2 cups brown sugar, the baking powder, baking soda, cinnamon and salt together. Combine the egg, buttermilk and oil in a mixing bowl and beat until smooth. Add the dry ingredients and mix just until moistened; the batter will be slightly lumpy. Fold in the cranberries.

Spoon into foil-lined muffin cups. Sprinkle with 2 tablespoons brown sugar. Bake at 375 degrees for 35 minutes. Cool for 5 minutes. Serve warm.

Makes 6

Angel Biscuits
Sister Schubert's Homemade Roll Bakery

1 envelope rapid-rising dry yeast
1/4 cup (105-degree) warm water
6 cups self-rising flour
2 teaspoons sugar
1 teaspoon baking soda

1 cup (2 sticks) butter, chilled
    and chopped
1/2 cup shortening, chilled
2 cups buttermilk, chilled
1/2 cup (4 ounces) sour cream, chilled

Stir the yeast into the warm water in a cup and let stand for 10 minutes or until foamy. Mix the flour, sugar and baking soda in a bowl. Cut in the butter and shortening until crumbly. Combine the yeast mixture with the buttermilk and sour cream in a bowl and mix well. Add to the crumbly mixture and mix to form a dough.

Roll the dough 3/4 inch thick on a lightly floured surface. Cut biscuits with a floured 2 1/2-inch cutter. Arrange on a baking sheet and let rise for 30 minutes. Bake at 420 degrees for 9 1/2 minutes.

Makes 27

Buttermilk Biscuits with Sausage Gravy

Buttermilk Biscuits

2 cups unbleached flour

1 tablespoon baking powder

1/2 teaspoon baking soda

1 teaspoon salt

6 tablespoons shortening

3/4 cup buttermilk

Sausage Gravy

1 pound bulk pork sausage

3 tablespoons bacon drippings

1/3 cup flour

3 cups milk

1/2 teaspoon salt

1/4 teaspoon black pepper

1/4 teaspoon red pepper flakes (optional)

To *prepare the biscuits*, mix the flour, baking powder, baking soda and salt together. Add the shortening and cut in with a pastry blender or fork to resemble coarse crumbs. Add the buttermilk and mix just until moistened; do not overmix.

Remove to a floured surface and sprinkle with additional flour. Knead 4 or 5 times. Roll 3/4 inch thick and cut with a floured 3-inch cutter.

Arrange the biscuits with edges almost touching on a baking sheet. Bake at 450 degrees for 12 to 14 minutes or until golden brown.

To *prepare the gravy*, brown the sausage in a large skillet, stirring until crumbly. Remove the sausage with a slotted spoon to drain, reserving the sausage drippings in the skillet. Add the bacon drippings and flour, mixing well. Cook until the flour is golden brown, stirring constantly. Whisk in the milk. Season with salt, black pepper and red pepper flakes.

Bring to a boil and reduce the heat to medium. Return the sausage to the skillet. Cook for 15 minutes or until thickened, stirring constantly. Serve with the biscuits.

Serves 6 to 8

Sweet Potato Biscuits

3 large sweet potatoes
1/4 cup milk
2 1/2 cups flour
4 teaspoons baking powder
2 tablespoons sugar

1/8 teaspoon cinnamon
1 teaspoon salt
1/4 teaspoon cayenne pepper
1/2 cup (1 stick) unsalted butter, chilled
   and chopped

Pierce the sweet potatoes with a fork and place on a baking sheet. Bake at 400 degrees for 1 hour or until tender; the juices will begin to seep from the sweet potatoes. Let stand until cool enough to handle and cut into halves. Scoop out the pulp and press through a sieve. Measure 1 3/4 cups sweet potato pulp. Combine with the milk in a bowl and whisk until smooth.

Mix the flour, baking powder, sugar, cinnamon, salt and cayenne pepper in a bowl. Cut in the butter with a pastry blender or 2 knives to resemble coarse crumbs. Add the sweet potato mixture and mix well. Knead 1 or 2 times on a lightly floured surface. Pat 1/2 inch thick and cut with a floured 2-inch cutter.

Arrange the biscuits on a parchment-lined baking sheet. Bake at 400 degrees for 20 minutes.

You can brush the biscuits with melted butter and sprinkle with cinnamon-sugar for a sweeter biscuit if desired.

Makes 1 dozen

The photograph for this recipe appears on page 46.

Crescent Rolls

½ cup shortening
1 teaspoon salt
1 cup boiling water
1 envelope dry yeast
3 tablespoons lukewarm water

2 eggs
½ cup sugar
4 cups (about) flour
softened butter

Combine the shortening and salt in a heatproof bowl and add the boiling water; stir to melt the shortening and dissolve the salt. Let stand until lukewarm. Dissolve the yeast in the lukewarm water in a cup.

Beat the eggs in a large mixing bowl. Add the sugar, shortening mixture and yeast mixture; mix well. Mix in 2 cups of the flour, then add enough of the remaining flour to make a workable dough. Knead several times to mix well. Place in a greased bowl, turning to coat the surface. Chill, covered, in the refrigerator for 3 hours or longer.

Divide the dough into 2 portions. Pat each into a circle ¼ inch thick. Spread with softened butter and cut each into 12 wedges. Roll up each wedge from the wide end. Arrange on a parchment-lined baking sheet.

Let rise in a warm place free from drafts until doubled in bulk. Bake at 375 degrees for 8 to 10 minutes or until golden brown.

Makes 2 dozen

Caribbean-Style Banana Bread

2 cups flour
1 teaspoon baking powder
1/2 teaspoon baking soda
1 1/2 teaspoons cinnamon
1/4 teaspoon salt
1/2 cup (1 stick) butter, softened
1/2 cup packed brown sugar
2 eggs, lightly beaten
1 teaspoon vanilla extract
1 cup mashed bananas
1/2 cup chopped macadamias
8 ounces cream cheese, softened
1 egg
1/4 cup packed brown sugar
1/2 cup flaked or shredded coconut

Grease the bottoms and 1/2 inch up the sides of 2 loaf pans. Mix the flour, baking powder, baking soda, cinnamon and salt together.

Cream the butter at high speed in a mixing bowl for 30 seconds. Add 1/2 cup brown sugar, 2 eggs and the vanilla and beat until smooth. Add the dry ingredients alternately with the bananas, beating at low speed until smooth after each addition. Stir in the macadamias.

Combine the cream cheese, 1 egg and 1/4 cup brown sugar in a mixing bowl and beat at medium speed until nearly smooth. Stir in the coconut.

Spoon 1/4 of the banana batter into each loaf pan. Spread 1/4 of the cream cheese mixture over the batter in each pan and cut through with a spatula to marbleize. Repeat with the remaining batter and cream cheese mixture, but do not cut through to marbleize.

Bake at 350 degrees for 50 minutes or until a wooden pick inserted into the center of the loaves comes out clean. Cool in the loaf pans on a wire rack for 10 minutes, then remove to the wire rack to cool completely.

Makes 2 loaves

Pumpkin Bread

3 cups sugar
1 cup vegetable oil
3 eggs
2 cups mashed cooked pumpkin
3 cups flour
1/2 teaspoon baking powder

1/2 teaspoon salt
1 teaspoon baking soda
1 teaspoon cinnamon
1 teaspoon ground cloves
1 teaspoon nutmeg
1/2 cup chopped pecans

Combine the sugar, oil, eggs and pumpkin in a mixing bowl and beat until smooth. Add the flour, baking powder, salt, baking soda, cinnamon, cloves and nutmeg, mixing well after each addition. Stir in the pecans.

Spoon into 2 greased and floured 7×9-inch loaf pans. Bake at 350 degrees for 1 hour. Cool in the pans for 10 minutes, then remove to a wire rack to cool completely. Serve with cream cheese.

Makes 2 loaves

Strawberry Honey Butter

1 pint fresh strawberries, stemmed
3 tablespoons honey
1 teaspoon sugar

1 teaspoon lime juice
3/4 cup (1 1/2 sticks) butter, softened

Process the strawberries in a food processor until smooth. Strain through a sieve into a saucepan. Add the honey, sugar and lime juice and mix well. Bring to a boil and cook for 3 minutes or until thickened, stirring constantly. Cool to room temperature.

Combine the strawberry mixture with the butter in a bowl and mix until smooth. Let stand, covered, for 1 hour before serving.

You may wrap the butter in waxed paper and store in the refrigerator for up to 2 days or in the freezer for up to 2 months.

Makes 1 1/2 cups

White Bread

5 tablespoons shortening
5 tablespoons sugar
1½ teaspoons salt
2 cups milk

2 eggs, beaten
1 teaspoon dry yeast
¼ cup lukewarm water
6¼ cups flour

Combine the shortening, sugar, salt and 1 cup of the milk in a saucepan; bring to a boil. Remove from the heat and add the remaining 1 cup milk, then stir in the eggs. Let stand until lukewarm. Dissolve the yeast in the lukewarm water. Add to the milk mixture and mix well.

Combine with the flour in a large bowl and mix to form a dough. Place in a greased bowl, turning to coat the surface. Let rise until doubled in bulk. Knead the dough until smooth and shape into loaves.

Place the loaves in greased loaf pans. Let rise until doubled in bulk. Bake at 350 degrees for 1 hour. Remove to a wire rack to cool completely.

Makes 2 loaves

Whole Wheat Bread

1 cup milk	1 cup lukewarm water
5 tablespoons molasses	5 cups whole wheat flour
2 teaspoons salt	1 cup all-purpose flour
1 envelope dry yeast	1 tablespoon melted shortening

Bring the milk just to a simmer in a saucepan and remove from the heat. Stir in the molasses and salt. Cool to lukewarm. Dissolve the yeast in the lukewarm water and let stand for several minutes. Add to the milk mixture and mix well.

Mix the whole wheat flour and all-purpose flour together. Add half the flour mixture to the milk mixture and beat until smooth. Add the melted shortening and remaining flour mixture and mix to form a dough. Knead until smooth. Place in a greased bowl, turning to coat the surface. Let rise in a warm place until doubled in bulk.

Punch down the dough and let rise again until ¾ the size of the previous rising. Shape into 2 balls of equal size and let rise for 10 to 15 minutes longer. Shape into loaves and place in greased loaf pans. Let rise until doubled in bulk.

Bake the loaves at 400 degrees for 15 minutes. Reduce the oven temperature to 325 degrees and bake until the loaves test done and are golden brown, covering with foil if necessary to prevent overbrowning.

Makes 2 loaves

Pita Bread

1 1/4 teaspoons dry yeast
1 cup lukewarm water
2 tablespoons honey or sugar

1 teaspoon salt
3 1/4 cups unbleached flour
olive oil or cornmeal

Sprinkle the yeast over the lukewarm water in a medium bowl. Let stand for 5 minutes. Stir in the honey. Add the salt and 3 cups of the flour 1 cup at a time, mixing well after each addition, and kneading when it becomes too stiff to stir. Knead in enough of the remaining 1/4 cup flour to make a smooth dough.

Place in a greased bowl, turning to coat the surface. Let rise, covered, in a warm place for 1 hour or until doubled in bulk. Punch down the dough and remove to a floured surface. Knead for 5 minutes. Divide into 12 equal portions. Knead each portion for several minutes and then flatten each into a circle 1/8 inch or less in thickness. Let rest for 30 minutes.

Preheat a baking sheet at 500 degrees. Brush the baking sheet with olive oil or sprinkle with cornmeal to prevent sticking. Arrange the dough circles on the baking sheet and bake for 6 to 8 minutes or until puffed and light brown. Cool on a wire rack for crisp bread. For a softer bread, wrap it in a damp cloth and place in a paper bag for 15 minutes.

Makes 1 dozen

HUMMUS

Combine one 16-ounce can drained chick-peas with 1/4 medium white onion, 1 large garlic clove, 1/2 cup pine nuts and 1/4 cup grated Parmesan cheese in a food processor and process to mix well. Add 1 tablespoon fresh lemon juice, 1 tablespoon tahini, 1/4 teaspoon salt, 1/2 teaspoon black pepper and 1/4 teaspoon cayenne pepper. Process until smooth. Chill in the refrigerator for 12 hours or longer. You can add chopped roasted red bell peppers if desired. Serve with pita bread for a healthy vegetarian source of protein.

Blue Corn Bread

3 tablespoons unsalted butter
3 tablespoons vegetable oil
¹/₄ cup chopped roasted red
   bell peppers
1 jalapeño chile, seeded and minced
¹/₄ cup yellow corn kernels
2 eggs

³/₄ cup buttermilk
1 cup blue cornmeal
³/₄ cup flour
1 tablespoon sugar
2 teaspoons baking powder
¹/₄ teaspoon baking soda
¹/₂ teaspoon salt

Melt the butter with the oil in a skillet. Add the roasted bell peppers, jalapeño chile and corn and sauté for 1 to 2 minutes. Beat the eggs with the buttermilk in a bowl. Add the sautéed vegetables and mix well.

Sift the cornmeal with the flour, sugar, baking powder, baking soda and salt. Fold into the vegetable mixture, mixing just until moistened.

Spoon into a greased 8×8-inch baking pan. Bake at 375 degrees for 45 to 50 minutes or until a wooden pick inserted into the center comes out clean. Cut into squares to serve.

Serves 8 *to* 10

SEASONING A CAST-IRON SKILLET

Wash the skillet well in warm soapy water and towel dry. Coat the skillet inside and out with canola oil, wiping away any excess oil. Place in a 350-degree oven for 30 minutes. Turn off the oven and let the skillet stand in the oven until cool enough to handle. It is ready to use, and the more you use it, the better it cooks. That is why cast-iron skillets are never discarded, but are often passed down in a family.

Mexican Corn Bread

1 pound hot bulk pork sausage
1 cup self-rising cornmeal
1 (8-ounce) can cream-style corn
1 onion, chopped
1 green bell pepper, chopped
3 or 4 jalapeño chiles, chopped

2 cups (8 ounces) shredded sharp
    Cheddar cheese
1 cup milk
¼ cup vegetable oil
3 eggs

Brown the sausage in a skillet, stirring until crumbly; drain. Combine with the cornmeal, corn, onion, bell pepper, jalapeño chiles and cheese in a bowl. Add the milk, oil and eggs and mix well.

Spoon into a 9×12-inch baking dish sprayed with nonstick cooking spray. Bake at 350 degrees for 1 hour and 20 minutes or until golden brown. Cut into squares to serve.

Serves 12

Beer Batter Hush Puppies

1½ cups self-rising cornmeal
¼ cup self-rising flour
2 small onions, finely chopped
1 medium green bell pepper,
    finely chopped
3 jalapeño chiles, finely chopped

1 tomato, finely chopped
1 egg, lightly beaten
1½ teaspoons Worcestershire sauce
⅛ teaspoon hot sauce
½ cup beer
vegetable oil for frying

Mix the cornmeal and flour in a large bowl. Add the onions, bell pepper, jalapeño chiles and tomato and mix well. Stir in the egg, Worcestershire sauce and hot sauce. Add the beer and mix well.

Heat 2 inches of oil in a small heavy saucepan. Drop the batter by rounded tablespoonfuls a few at a time into the hot oil. Fry for 1 to 2 minutes or until golden brown, turning once. Drain on paper towels.

Makes 3½ dozen

Black Bean Soup with Cilantro Lime Sour Cream

Soup

1 pound dried black beans	1/3 cup packed chopped flat-leaf parsley
3/4 cup finely chopped celery	1 1/2 tablespoons minced garlic
3/4 cup finely chopped onion	2 jalapeño chiles, minced
3/4 cup finely chopped leeks	1 tablespoon red wine vinegar
2 tablespoons olive oil	2 teaspoons ground cumin
10 cups chicken broth	1 teaspoon ground coriander
1 large tomato, chopped	salt and pepper to taste
1 cup packed chopped cilantro	

Cilantro Lime Sour Cream

2 teaspoons fresh lemon juice	1/2 cup chopped cilantro
2 teaspoons fresh lime juice	salt and pepper to taste
3/4 cup (6 ounces) sour cream	

To *prepare the soup*, combine the beans with enough water to cover by 3 inches in a large bowl. Let stand for 8 hours; drain, rinse and drain again.

Sauté the celery, onion and leeks in the olive oil in a large heavy saucepan over medium heat for 10 minutes or until the vegetables are tender. Add the beans, chicken broth, tomato, cilantro, parsley, garlic, jalapeño chiles, vinegar, cumin and coriander. Bring the soup to a boil and reduce the heat to medium-low. Simmer, covered, for 2 hours or until the beans are very tender, stirring occasionally.

Process the soup to the desired consistency in batches in a blender or food processor. Combine the batches in the saucepan and season with salt and pepper to taste. Heat to serving temperature.

To *prepare the sour cream*, combine the lemon juice, lime juice, sour cream and cilantro in a bowl and mix well. Season with salt and pepper to taste.

Ladle the soup into serving bowls. Serve with a dollop of the sour cream, additional chopped cilantro, tomato and red onion.

You may prepare the soup a day in advance and chill until time to reheat and serve.

Serves 8

Crawfish Bisque
Gourmet Entrées to Go

1 cup chopped red bell pepper
1 cup chopped green bell pepper
1 cup chopped red onion
1 cup chopped celery
1/2 cup olive oil
3/4 cup flour
4 cups chicken stock

2 cups heavy cream
2 tablespoons chopped garlic
1 1/2 tablespoons Cajun seasoning
1/2 teaspoon thyme
1 to 1 1/2 pounds crawfish, cooked
chopped green onions

Sauté the bell peppers, onion and celery in the olive oil in a heavy saucepan over medium-high heat for 2 minutes or until tender. Sprinkle the flour over the vegetables. Cook until the flour is incorporated and bubbly, stirring constantly.

Add the chicken stock, cream, garlic, Cajun seasoning and thyme. Simmer until slightly thickened, stirring constantly. Stir in the crawfish and simmer until heated through. Ladle into soup bowls and garnish with green onions.

Serves 8 to 10

Oyster Brie Soup

1/2 cup (1 stick) butter
3/4 cup chopped onion
1/2 cup chopped celery
2 garlic cloves, crushed
1/2 cup (1 stick) butter
1/2 cup flour
2 pounds Brie cheese, rind removed
   and cubed

5 cups water
2 cups cream
3 dozen small oysters with liquor
1/2 teaspoon salt
1/2 teaspoon cayenne pepper
1/2 teaspoon white pepper

Melt 1/2 cup butter in a large saucepan. Add the onion, celery and garlic and sauté until tender. Melt 1/2 cup butter in a small saucepan over low heat. Add the flour and cook for 2 minutes, stirring constantly. Add to the vegetable mixture and mix well.

Stir in the cubed Brie cheese, water, cream and undrained oysters. Simmer until the soup is thickened and the edges of the oysters curl, stirring constantly. Season with the salt, cayenne pepper and white pepper. Ladle into soup bowls.

Serves 8 to 10

Redfish Soup

5 tablespoons butter
5 tablespoons flour
2 cups chopped onions
1 cup chopped celery
3/4 cup chopped green bell pepper
3 garlic cloves, minced
3 cups drained canned tomatoes
1/2 (6-ounce) can tomato paste
2 1/2 cups chicken stock

1/2 cup chopped green onions
1/2 cup chopped parsley
2 teaspoons lemon juice
Tabasco sauce to taste
4 bay leaves
1/2 teaspoon thyme
2 teaspoons salt
1/2 teaspoon pepper
2 1/2 pounds redfish fillets

Melt the butter in a heavy saucepan. Add the flour and cook over low heat until light brown, stirring constantly. Add the onions, celery, bell pepper and garlic. Cook for 10 minutes or until the vegetables are light brown, stirring occasionally.

Combine the tomatoes, tomato paste and chicken stock in a bowl and mix well. Add to the soup and cook for 5 minutes, stirring constantly. Stir in the green onions, parsley, lemon juice, Tabasco sauce, bay leaves, thyme, salt and pepper. Simmer for 45 minutes.

Add the fish and simmer for 10 to 15 minutes longer or until the fish flakes easily. Discard the bay leaves. Ladle into soup bowls and serve with warm French bread and a green salad.

Serves 6

Seafood Gumbo
Dewey Destin Seafood Restaurant

²/₃ cup flour
²/₃ cup vegetable oil
2 cups chopped onions
1 cup chopped celery
¹/₂ cup chopped green bell pepper
¹/₂ cup chopped green onion tops
¹/₄ cup chopped parsley
4 garlic cloves, minced

hot water
1 tablespoon salt
1 teaspoon cayenne pepper
6 cups hot water
2 pounds uncooked shrimp, peeled
1 pound crab claw meat
1 pint oysters in liquor, or 8 ounces
    cooked grouper fillets

Blend the flour and oil in a 4-cup glass measure. Microwave on High for 6 minutes. Stir to mix well. Microwave for 30 to 60 seconds longer or until the roux is a dark caramel color, stirring every 30 seconds.

Add the onions, celery and bell pepper. Microwave on High for 3 minutes. Stir to mix well. Add the green onion tops, parsley and garlic. Microwave for 2 minutes.

Add enough hot water to measure 4 cups. Pour into a 5-quart microwave-safe dish. Add the salt, cayenne pepper and 6 cups hot water. Microwave, covered, on High for 15 minutes.

Stir in the shrimp and crab meat. Microwave, covered, on Medium for 20 minutes. Add the undrained oysters and microwave on Medium for 10 minutes longer. Serve with rice and filé.

You may prepare the roux in the microwave to save time and finish the gumbo on the stovetop if preferred.

Serves 8 to10

The photograph for this recipe appears on page 74.

Caramelized Onion Soup

2 tablespoons extra-virgin olive oil
3 red onions, coarsely chopped
3 white onions, coarsely chopped
3 yellow onions, coarsely chopped
12 fresh pearl onions
3 shallots, coarsely chopped
2 leeks, sliced ¼ inch thick

½ cup coarsely chopped chives
¼ cup marsala
6 cups beef stock
2 tablespoons coarsely chopped dried
    porcini mushrooms
1 tablespoon fresh thyme
fresh thyme sprigs

Heat the olive oil in a 4-quart saucepan. Add the red onions, white onions, yellow onions, pearl onions and shallots. Sauté until the onions are golden brown and tender. Add the leeks and chives and sauté for 5 minutes longer or until deep golden brown.

Stir in the wine and cook for 2 minutes or until bubbly, stirring frequently. Add the beef stock 2 cups at a time and cook for 15 minutes after each addition or until the liquid is reduced by ¼; add the mushrooms and thyme with the last addition of stock. Ladle into soup bowls and garnish with thyme sprigs.

Serves 4

Potato Leek Soup

6 large leek bulbs, thinly sliced
¼ cup (½ stick) butter
8 medium Yukon Gold potatoes, peeled
  and thinly sliced

1 tablespoon salt
5 cups chicken stock
2 cups half-and-half
pepper to taste

Sauté the leeks in the butter in a saucepan over low heat for 10 minutes. Add the potatoes and salt. Cook, covered, over low heat until the potatoes are tender. Process in a food processor until smooth.

Combine the chicken stock and half-and-half in a saucepan and bring just to a simmer. Stir in the potato purée. Cook until heated through. Adjust the salt and season with pepper to taste. Ladle into soup bowls.

You may also chill the soup in the refrigerator. Stir in 1 cup heavy cream at serving time and serve cold.

Serves 6 to 8

LEEKS

Leeks, sweet and moderately flavored members of the onion family, are long and cylindrical with a pale white root end and dark green leaves. One should select small- to medium-size firm, unblemished leeks. To use leeks, remove the leaf ends or whole leaves with a knife and trim off the roots. Starting one inch from the root end, slit the leek lengthwise. Swish in a basin or sink of cold water until all dirt has been removed. Cut crosswise to slice or chop into smaller pieces if desired.

Chicken Tortilla Soup

2 garlic cloves, minced
2 tablespoons butter or margarine
2 (14-ounce) cans chicken broth
2 (14-ounce) cans stewed tomatoes,
coarsely chopped
2 cups chopped cooked chicken
1 cup salsa

2½ teaspoons cumin
1 cup coarsely chopped cilantro
3 cups corn tortilla strips or baked
tortilla chips
2 avocados, chopped
4 to 8 ounces Monterey Jack cheese,
cut into ¼-inch cubes (optional)

Sauté the garlic in the butter in a saucepan for 3 minutes. Stir in the chicken broth, tomatoes, chicken, salsa and cumin. Bring to a boil and reduce the heat. Simmer for 20 minutes. Remove from the heat and stir in the cilantro. Place the tortilla strips, avocados and cheese in soup bowls and ladle the soup into the bowls.

Serves 6 to 8

Wild Rice Soup

½ cup (1 stick) butter
1 large onion, finely chopped
3 cups chopped celery with leaves
8 ounces mushrooms, chopped
1 tablespoon minced garlic
¼ cup (½ stick) butter
¼ cup flour

1 teaspoon salt
½ teaspoon pepper
2½ cups milk
1½ cups half-and-half
1¾ cups cooked wild rice
chopped fresh chives

Melt ½ cup butter in a skillet. Add the onion and sauté until tender. Add the celery, mushrooms and garlic. Sauté until the vegetables are tender. Melt ¼ cup butter in a heavy saucepan. Add the flour, salt and pepper and cook for 1 minute or until bubbly, stirring constantly. Stir in the milk and half-and-half gradually. Cook over medium heat until thickened, stirring constantly. Add the vegetables and rice to the saucepan. Reduce the heat to low and simmer for 15 minutes. Ladle into soup bowls and garnish with chives.

Serves 8

The photograph for this recipe appears on page 74.

Corn and Sausage Chowder

1 pound mild bulk pork sausage
1 large onion, chopped
3 large potatoes, peeled and cubed
2 cups water
1 teaspoon basil
2 teaspoons salt, or to taste

1/2 teaspoon pepper
1 (17-ounce) can cream-style corn
1 (16-ounce) can whole kernel
    corn, drained
1 (12-ounce) can evaporated milk

Shape the sausage into a large patty. Brown on both sides in a large skillet for 5 minutes. Remove the patty to drain and drain the skillet, reserving 2 tablespoons of the drippings. Add the onion to the drippings in the skillet and sauté until tender.

Crumble the sausage patty into a saucepan. Add the onion, potatoes, water, basil, salt and pepper. Bring to a boil and reduce the heat to low. Simmer, covered, for 15 minutes or until the potatoes are tender. Stir in the corn and evaporated milk. Cook, covered, until heated through. Ladle into soup bowls.

Serves 6

Chilled Avocado and Cucumber Soup

2 avocados, coarsely chopped
2 cucumbers, peeled, seeded and
    coarsely chopped
2 tablespoons chopped onion
garlic to taste
2 cups chicken stock

1 cup (8 ounces) sour cream
juice of 1 lemon
3 dashes of Tabasco sauce
minced fresh dill weed to taste
salt, cayenne pepper and black pepper
    to taste

Combine the avocados, cucumbers, onion and garlic in a food processor. Add the chicken stock, sour cream, lemon juice, Tabasco sauce, dill weed, salt, cayenne pepper and black pepper to taste. Process until smooth. Spoon into a bowl and chill until serving time.

Serves 4

Caper Steak Salad Sandwich

2 cups (½-inch) cooked steak cubes
2 tablespoons drained capers
2 tablespoons chopped gherkins
2 tablespoons minced red onion
3 tablespoons mayonnaise
2 tablespoons Dijon mustard

salt and pepper to taste
8 (½-inch) slices rosemary or other
  herbed country bread
3 tablespoons mayonnaise
8 tomato slices
2 small bunches arugula, trimmed

Combine the steak, capers, gherkins, onion, 3 tablespoons mayonnaise and the Dijon mustard in a medium bowl and toss to mix well. Season with salt and pepper to taste.

Spread 1 side of each bread slice with some of the remaining 3 tablespoons mayonnaise. Spread the steak salad on 4 of the bread slices and top each with 2 slices of the tomato, the arugula and the remaining bread slices. Serve immediately or store, covered, in the refrigerator until serving time.

Serves 4

Pesto Mayonnaise Chicken Sandwich

¼ cup prepared pesto
¼ cup mayonnaise
1 thin baguette
2 poached or roasted chicken breasts

Bibb lettuce
½ red onion, thinly sliced and separated
  into rings
grated Parmesan cheese

Combine the pesto and mayonnaise in a bowl and mix until smooth. Cut the baguette into halves horizontally. Spread the pesto mayonnaise on the cut sides. Cut the chicken into very thin slices and arrange on the bottom baguette half. Layer lettuce and the onion on the chicken and sprinkle with Parmesan cheese. Top with the remaining baguette half and cut into servings.

Serves 4 to 6

The photograph for this recipe appears on page 86.

Fried Oyster Po' Boys

2 dozen large oysters
1 teaspoon garlic powder
1 1/2 tablespoons salt
2 teaspoons black pepper
1/2 teaspoon cayenne pepper
5 eggs, beaten

2 cups cornmeal
salt and black pepper to taste
vegetable oil for deep-frying
3 loaves Po' Boy bread or French bread
1/4 cup (1/2 stick) butter, melted
Creole Tartar Sauce (below)

Drain the oysters and pat dry. Sprinkle with the garlic powder, 1 1/2 tablespoons salt, 2 teaspoons black pepper, and the cayenne pepper. Dip the oysters into the eggs and then roll in the cornmeal, coating well. Sprinkle with additional salt and black pepper. Chill in the refrigerator for 2 hours.

Dip the oysters again into the eggs and roll again in the cornmeal. Deep-fry in 360-degree oil until golden brown, turning several times. Drain on paper towels.

Cut the bread loaves into halves lengthwise. Brush with the butter and bake or grill until the edges begin to brown. Spread the cut sides with the desired amount of Creole Tartar Sauce. Arrange the oysters on the bottom bread halves and top with the remaining bread halves. Serve immediately.

Serves 3

CREOLE TARTAR SAUCE

Combine 1 cup dill pickle relish, 6 thinly sliced green onions, 2 teaspoons prepared horseradish and 2 tablespoons Cajun seasoning in a bowl and toss to mix. Add 1 1/2 tablespoons coarse Creole mustard, 1 1/2 teaspoons Tabasco sauce and 1 cup mayonnaise and mix well. Serve on po' boys, with fried seafood, or as a dip for vegetables.

Grilled Portobello Sandwiches

Basil Horseradish Mayonnaise

1 cup mayonnaise
1/3 cup chopped fresh basil
2 tablespoons prepared horseradish
1 teaspoon lemon juice
1/2 teaspoon salt
1/2 teaspoon pepper

Sandwiches

1/3 cup olive oil
1 tablespoon minced garlic
1 medium purple onion, cut into 6 slices
6 large portobello mushroom caps
6 gourmet buns, or 12 slices hearty
     gourmet bread
6 leaves Boston lettuce or romaine
2 Roma tomatoes, cut into 6 slices each

To *prepare the mayonnaise*, combine the mayonnaise with the basil, horseradish, lemon juice, salt and pepper in a bowl and mix until smooth.

To *prepare the sandwiches*, whisk together the olive oil and garlic in a small bowl. Brush on both sides of the onion slices and mushroom caps. Heat a covered grill to 350 to 400 degrees. Add the onions and mushroom caps and grill for 4 minutes on each side or until tender.

Cut the bread into halves lengthwise. Grill cut side down for 2 minutes or until light brown. Spread the mayonnaise on the bread. Layer the lettuce, onion, mushroom caps and tomatoes on half the bread and top with the remaining bread.

You may wrap the sandwiches in parchment and tie with raffia for a picnic or tailgate.

Serves 6

Spinach Salad

Spiced Pecans

¹/₃ **cup honey**	¹/₄ **teaspoon ginger**
1 **tablespoon water**	¹/₈ **teaspoon salt**
1 **tablespoon sugar**	2 **cups pecan halves**
¹/₂ **teaspoon cinnamon**	

Salad

1 **(6-ounce) can frozen cranberry juice** **concentrate, thawed**	1 **cup dried cranberries**
	¹/₈ **teaspoon salt**
¹/₃ **cup olive oil**	4 **cups sliced unpeeled apples**
3 **tablespoons raspberry vinaigrette or** **raspberry vinegar**	8 **cups torn spinach**
	1 **cup thinly sliced celery**

To *prepare the pecans*, combine the honey, water, sugar, cinnamon, ginger and salt in a bowl and mix well. Add the pecans and toss to coat evenly. Spread in a shallow baking pan. Bake at 350 degrees for 16 minutes, stirring several times. Let stand until cool. Bake for several minutes longer if the pecans are still sticky. Store in an airtight container.

To *prepare the salad*, combine the cranberry juice concentrate, olive oil, raspberry vinaigrette, dried cranberries and salt in a bowl and mix well. Pour over the apples in a shallow dish. Chill, covered, for 24 hours, stirring several times. Combine the spinach and celery in a salad bowl. Add the apple mixture and spiced pecans; toss to mix.

Serves 8

The photograph for this recipe appears on page 74.

BEAUTY WITH YOUR GREENS

Add edible flowers to your salad greens for a colorful presentation. Many well-known flowers are edible, but it is important to choose varieties free of chemicals and pesticides.

Chive blossoms impart a light and oniony flavor. Lilac has a lemony taste with floral overtones. Marigolds resemble saffron, with a citrus-like flavor of lemon and tangerine. Nasturtiums are peppery like watercress and are the most commonly used edible flower. Pansies are slightly sweet. Roses are reminiscent of strawberries and green apples, with a subtle undertone. Snapdragons have a melon flavor. Violets impart a sweet perfumed flavor.

Berries-Go-Tropical Salad

1 cup thawed frozen
   lemonade concentrate
1/4 cup honey
2 tablespoons vegetable oil
2 papayas
2 or 3 mangoes

4 kiwifruit, peeled and chopped
1 cup fresh raspberries
1 cup fresh blackberries
1 cup fresh strawberries,
   cut into quarters
poppy seeds (optional)

Combine the lemonade concentrate with the honey and oil in a small bowl or cruet. Stir or shake to mix well.

Peel the papayas and mangoes and cut into bite-size pieces, discarding the seeds. Combine with the kiwifruit, raspberries, blackberries and strawberries in a large bowl. Chill until serving time. Add the dressing to the fruit at serving time and toss gently to coat well. Sprinkle with poppy seeds.

Serves 8 to 10

The photograph for this recipe appears on page 74.

Strawberry Pretzel Salad

2 1/2 cups crushed pretzels
3/4 cup (1 1/2 sticks) margarine, softened
1/4 cup packed brown sugar
1 (6-ounce) package strawberry gelatin
2 cups boiling water

1 (10-ounce) package frozen strawberries
8 ounces cream cheese, softened
1 cup sugar
8 ounces whipped topping

Mix the pretzels, margarine and brown sugar in a bowl. Press over the bottom of a 9×13-inch baking dish. Bake at 350 degrees for 10 minutes. Cool to room temperature. Dissolve the gelatin in the boiling water. Add the frozen strawberries to the warm gelatin mixture, stirring to separate the berries. Chill until the mixture begins to set. Beat the cream cheese and sugar in a mixing bowl until smooth. Fold in the whipped topping. Spread over the pretzel layer. Spoon the strawberry mixture over the top. Chill until firm. Cut into squares.

Serves 10 to 12

Fig Salad

1 (9-ounce) package dried figs, about 24 figs
1 bottle white wine

8 ounces cream cheese, softened
1 (2½-ounce) package black walnuts
1 head romaine

Combine the dried figs with the wine in a bowl and mix well. Let stand for 20 minutes; drain. Combine the cream cheese and walnuts in a bowl and mix well. Spoon the cream cheese mixture into the figs. Arrange on a plate lined with the romaine.

Serves 6

Asian Salad

Asian Dressing

⅓ cup rice wine vinegar
2 tablespoons soy sauce
1 garlic clove, minced
1 teaspoon sugar

¼ teaspoon ground ginger
¼ teaspoon red pepper flakes or chili paste
¾ cup vegetable oil

Salad

1 head red leaf lettuce, torn
¼ cup cilantro leaves
1 yellow bell pepper, thinly sliced into rings

⅓ cup unsalted dry-roasted peanuts, finely chopped (optional)

To prepare the dressing, combine the vinegar, soy sauce, garlic, sugar, ginger and red pepper flakes in a bowl and mix well. Add the oil in a fine stream, whisking constantly until smooth.

To prepare the salad, toss the lettuce with the cilantro in a bowl. Add just enough of the dressing to coat lightly. Top with the bell pepper rings and sprinkle with the peanuts. Drizzle with additional dressing if desired; store any unused dressing in the refrigerator.

Serves 6

Caesar Salad
Seagars

Caesar Dressing

2 teaspoons minced garlic
2 teaspoons minced anchovy
2 teaspoons Dijon mustard
dash each of Worcestershire sauce and
    Tabasco sauce

4 egg yolks
1 cup blended olive oil
juice of 2 lemons
salt and pepper to taste

Salad

2 heads romaine, chopped
2 tablespoons (1 ounce) grated
    asiago cheese
2 cups (heaping) croutons

2 tablespoons (1 ounce) grated
    asiago cheese
freshly cracked pepper to taste

To *prepare the dressing*, combine the garlic, anchovy, Dijon mustard, Worcestershire sauce, Tabasco sauce and egg yolks in a wooden salad bowl and whisk until smooth. Add the olive oil in a fine stream, whisking constantly until emulsified. Add the lemon juice and season with salt and pepper, whisking to mix well.

To *prepare the salad*, swirl the dressing around the bowl to coat evenly. Add the romaine, 2 tablespoons asiago cheese and the croutons and toss to coat evenly. Spoon onto serving plates and top with 2 tablespoons asiago cheese and freshly cracked pepper.

You may use the Homemade Croutons (below) for the croutons in this recipe.

To avoid the possibility of salmonella from uncooked egg yolks, you can use an equivalent amount of egg yolk substitute.

Serves 4

HOMEMADE CROUTONS

Cut day-old bread into bite-size cubes. Combine with 1 teaspoon minced parsley and 2 minced garlic cloves in a large bowl. Drizzle with 5 to 6 tablespoons olive oil and sprinkle with salt and cayenne pepper to taste. Spread on a baking sheet and bake at 250 degrees for 1 hour and 20 minutes or until golden brown, stirring several times. Cool to room temperature and store in an airtight container. You can use cookie cutters to cut the bread into shapes appropriate for holiday or celebration salads.

Cucumber Slaw

3 or 4 cucumbers, peeled, seeded and
    thinly sliced
1/2 green bell pepper, chopped
1/2 red bell pepper, chopped
1 large Vidalia onion, chopped

1/2 cup cider vinegar
3/4 cup sugar
2 teaspoons celery seeds
1/2 teaspoon salt
1/2 teaspoon white pepper

Mix the cucumbers, bell peppers and onion gently in a large bowl. Combine the vinegar, sugar, celery seeds, salt and white pepper in a saucepan. Cook over medium heat until the sugar dissolves, stirring constantly. Add the dressing mixture to the cucumber mixture and toss to mix well. Chill for 1 to 2 hours before serving.

Serves 8

Lemon Basil Potato Salad

1/4 cup fresh lemon juice
1 tablespoon Dijon mustard
4 garlic cloves, minced
3/4 cup slivered fresh basil
salt and pepper to taste
2/3 cup olive oil
2 1/2 pounds red new potatoes,
    cut into quarters

vegetable oil or cooking spray
1 red onion, chopped
1 package fresh spinach, cut into strips
10 slices bacon, crisp-cooked
    and crumbled

Combine the lemon juice, Dijon mustard, garlic, basil, salt and pepper in a bowl. Add the olive oil in a fine stream, whisking constantly until smooth. Drizzle the potatoes with a small amount of vegetable oil in a bowl, tossing to coat lightly. Spread on a baking sheet. Bake at 475 degrees for 20 minutes or until tender, stirring frequently.

    Combine the potatoes with the onion and half the dressing mixture in a bowl; toss to coat well. Spoon the spinach into serving bowls or onto plates and drizzle with the remaining dressing mixture. Top with the potato mixture and sprinkle with the bacon.

Serves 6

Fresh Vegetable Potato Salad

Horseradish Dressing

$1/3$ cup cider vinegar
2 tablespoons prepared horseradish
$3/4$ cup mayonnaise
$3/4$ cup plain yogurt or sour cream
2 teaspoons dry mustard
1 teaspoon tarragon

$1/2$ cup minced fresh parsley
$1/4$ cup minced fresh dill weed,
   or 1 tablespoon dried dill weed
$1 1/2$ teaspoons salt
$1/2$ teaspoon freshly ground pepper

Salad

8 medium potatoes
3 hard-cooked eggs, chopped
1 red bell pepper, chopped
4 green onions with tops, minced
$2/3$ cup finely chopped seeded
   peeled cucumber

$1/3$ cup finely chopped carrots
$1/2$ cup toasted sunflower seeds
$1/2$ cup cherry tomato quarters
$1/4$ cup kalamata olives

To *prepare the dressing*, combine the vinegar, horseradish, mayonnaise, yogurt, dry mustard, tarragon, parsley, dill weed, salt and pepper in a bowl and mix well.

To *prepare the salad*, cut the potatoes into $1 1/2$-inch pieces. Combine with enough water to cover in a saucepan. Cook for 25 minutes or until fork-tender; drain and cool to room temperature. Combine the potatoes with the eggs, bell pepper, green onions, cucumber and carrots in a bowl.

Add the dressing to the potato mixture and mix gently to coat well. Chill until serving time. Add the sunflower seeds just before serving and mix gently. Garnish with the cherry tomatoes and kalamata olives.

Serves 8 to 10

The photograph for this recipe appears on page 74.

Bread Salad Tuscan Style
Rutherfords 465

1 pound plum tomatoes, seeded
   and chopped
1 pound European cucumbers, seeded
   and chopped
1 pound red onions, thinly sliced
2 bunches basil, slivered
4 garlic cloves, minced

6 tablespoons red wine vinegar
10 tablespoons extra-virgin olive oil
salt and pepper to taste
1 pound day-old bread, cubed
shaved Parmesan cheese
extra-virgin olive oil

Combine the tomatoes, cucumbers, onions, basil and garlic in a large bowl. Add the vinegar and 10 tablespoons olive oil and mix gently. Season with salt and pepper to taste. Add the bread cubes at serving time and toss gently.

Spoon onto a serving plate and sprinkle with Parmesan cheese. Drizzle with additional olive oil. Serve immediately.

Serves 10 *to* 12

Pasta Salad

1 (14-ounce) can artichoke
   hearts, drained
1 tablespoon olive oil
1 tablespoon water
1 tablespoon lemon juice
1 garlic clove, minced
$1/4$ teaspoon basil

$1/2$ teaspoon oregano
$1/4$ teaspoon pepper
3 cups cooked rotini
$2^1/2$ cups thinly sliced spinach
$1^1/4$ cups chopped seeded tomatoes
$1/2$ cup (2 ounces) crumbled feta cheese

Place 2 artichoke hearts in a food processor or blender for the dressing; reserve the remaining artichoke hearts for the salad. Add the olive oil, water, lemon juice, garlic, basil, oregano and pepper to the food processor; process until smooth.

Chop the reserved artichoke hearts. Combine with the pasta, spinach and tomatoes in a large bowl. Add the dressing and toss to coat evenly. Chill, covered, for 2 to 4 hours. Sprinkle with the cheese at serving time.

Serves 12

Bacon and Asparagus Pasta Salad

1 (16-ounce) package gemelli or other
   spiral pasta
1 large bunch asparagus
1 pound thick-sliced bacon,
   crisp-cooked and crumbled

3 to 4 tablespoons olive oil
1 cup (1/2-inch) cubes fresh buffalo
   mozzarella cheese
1 tablespoon crushed red pepper flakes
salt and freshly ground pepper to taste

Cook the pasta using the package directions; drain and cool slightly. Cut the asparagus diagonally into 2-inch pieces. Cook in a small amount of water in a saucepan for 8 to 10 minutes or until tender-crisp; drain. Combine the pasta, asparagus, bacon, olive oil, cheese and red pepper flakes in a bowl and toss gently to mix well. Season with salt and pepper. Serve immediately. You may prepare the salad in advance, adding 2 additional tablespoons olive oil and reserving the bacon to add at serving time. Do not reheat to serve, as the cheese will melt.

Serves 6 to 8

Cajun Red Beans and Rice Salad

Cajun Dressing

3 tablespoons vegetable oil
3 tablespoons vinegar
1 teaspoon hot sauce
2 to 3 teaspoons chili powder

1/2 teaspoon seasoned salt
1/4 teaspoon salt
1/4 teaspoon pepper

Salad

3 cups chilled cooked rice
1 (16-ounce) can red beans, drained
1 large tomato, chopped

1/2 cup chopped green bell pepper
1/2 cup chopped red onion
1 garlic clove, minced

To *prepare the dressing*, combine the oil, vinegar, hot sauce, chili powder, seasoned salt, salt and pepper in a jar with a tight-fitting lid. Shake to blend well.

   To *prepare the salad*, combine the rice, beans, tomato, bell pepper, onion and garlic in a large bowl and mix well. Add the dressing and toss to coat evenly. Chill, covered, for 1 hour.

Serves 12

Southwestern Lobster Salad

Rutherfords 465

Southwestern Dressing

¹/₂ **cup chopped onion**	¹/₄ **cup light vinegar**
1 **teaspoon chopped garlic**	¹/₄ **cup packed brown sugar**
1 **ounce ground cumin**	1 **chipotle chile**
¹/₄ **cup (¹/₂ stick) butter**	2 **bunches cilantro**
2 **egg yolks**	**salt to taste**
juice of 5 limes	4 **cups canola oil**

Salad

8 **ounces grilled fresh corn kernels**	8 **Roma tomatoes, sliced**
8 **ounces cooked black beans**	4 **flour tortillas, cut into strips and**
8 **cups mixed salad greens**	**crisp-fried**
cooked meat from 4 lobsters	**cilantro sprigs**

To prepare the dressing, sauté the onion and garlic with the cumin in the butter in a sauté pan for 4 minutes. Spoon into a blender. Add the egg yolks, lime juice, vinegar, brown sugar, chipotle chile, cilantro and salt. Add the canola oil in a steady stream, processing constantly at the lowest speed until smooth. Chill in the refrigerator.

To prepare the salad, combine the corn, beans and salad greens in a bowl. Add the desired amount of dressing and toss to coat well. Spoon onto a serving platter and top with the lobster meat. Arrange the sliced tomato around the edge and sprinkle with the tortilla strips and sprigs of cilantro.

Store any unused dressing in the refrigerator.

To avoid the possibility of salmonella from uncooked egg yolks, you can use an equivalent amount of egg yolk substitute in the dressing.

Serves 8

Niçoise Salad

Niçoise Vinaigrette

$^1/_4$ cup white wine vinegar
1 teaspoon Dijon mustard
$^1/_2$ teaspoon salt

$^1/_4$ teaspoon freshly ground pepper
$^3/_4$ cup olive oil

Salad

4 pounds (1-inch) sushi-quality
   yellowfin tuna steaks
olive oil
salt and freshly ground pepper to taste
arugula
1 pound green beans, trimmed and
   steamed or blanched

Vinaigrette Potato Salad (page 97)
4 tomatoes, cut into wedges
8 hard-cooked eggs, cut into halves
8 ounces kalamata olives or other
   black olives
1 can anchovies (optional)

To prepare the vinaigrette, combine the vinegar, Dijon mustard, salt and pepper in a bowl. Add the olive oil gradually, whisking constantly until emulsified.

   To prepare the salad, brush the tuna with olive oil and sprinkle with salt and pepper. Grill over hot coals for 2 minutes on each side; the center will be rare.

   Arrange arugula on a large platter. Top with the tuna, green beans, Vinaigrette Potato Salad, tomatoes, eggs, olives and anchovies. Drizzle with the vinaigrette.

Serves 8

Vinaigrette Potato Salad

Dijon Vinaigrette

3 tablespoons white wine vinegar or
    Champagne vinegar
$^1/_2$ teaspoon Dijon mustard

$^1/_2$ teaspoon salt
$^1/_4$ teaspoon freshly ground pepper
$^3/_4$ cup olive oil

Salad

1 pound small red new potatoes
1 pound small white boiling potatoes
salt to taste
$2^1/_2$ tablespoons dry white wine
2 tablespoons chicken stock
$^1/_4$ cup minced green onions

2 tablespoons minced fresh dill weed
2 tablespoons minced flat-leaf parsley
$2^1/_2$ tablespoons slivered basil
$1^1/_2$ teaspoons salt
$^1/_2$ teaspoon freshly ground pepper

To *prepare the vinaigrette*, combine the vinegar, Dijon mustard, salt and pepper in a small bowl. Add the olive oil gradually, whisking constantly until emulsified.

To *prepare the salad*, combine the potatoes with enough salted water to cover in a large saucepan. Bring to a boil and cook for 20 to 30 minutes or until tender; drain. Let stand, covered, in the saucepan for 10 minutes longer. Cool the potatoes until they are cool enough to handle and cut into halves or quarters. Combine with the wine and chicken stock in a bowl and toss lightly. Add the vinaigrette to the potatoes and mix gently. Add the green onions, dill weed, parsley, basil, salt and pepper and toss to mix well.

Serves 8

Grilled Chicken Fruit Salad

Apricot Vinaigrette

½ cup apricot preserves
¼ cup raspberry vinegar
2 tablespoons olive oil

2 tablespoons chopped cilantro
1 jalapeño chile, seeded and chopped

Salad

¾ cup apricot preserves
3 tablespoons soy sauce
3 tablespoons lemon juice
6 boneless skinless chicken breasts
1 fresh pineapple, peeled, cored and
   sliced 1 inch thick

2 heads Bibb lettuce, chopped
1 (11-ounce) can mandarin oranges,
   drained
2 cups fresh strawberry halves
1 cup fresh raspberries

To *prepare the vinaigrette*, combine the apricot preserves with the raspberry vinegar, olive oil, cilantro and jalapeño chile in a bowl and mix well.

To *prepare the salad*, combine the apricot preserves with the soy sauce and lemon juice in a bowl and mix well. Add the chicken and stir to coat evenly. Marinate in the refrigerator for 2 hours or longer; drain.

Place the chicken and pineapple slices on the grill and grill until cooked through. Place the lettuce on chilled serving plates. Place 1 chicken breast on each plate and top with the pineapple, mandarin oranges, strawberries and raspberries.

Drizzle with the vinaigrette. Serve with a glass of pinot grigio and crusty French bread.

Serves 6

WALNUT VINAIGRETTE

Blend ¼ cup Champagne vinegar and 2 tablespoons Dijon mustard in a small bowl. Whisk in ½ cup peanut oil, ½ cup olive oil and ¼ cup walnut oil. Stir in ¼ cup grated Parmesan cheese and season with salt and pepper to taste. Chill until serving time.

Roquefort Peppercorn Dressing

3/4 cup plus 2 tablespoons (3 1/2 ounces)
    crumbled Roquefort cheese
1 large garlic clove, crushed
1/2 cup mayonnaise

1/3 cup sour cream
1 tablespoon freshly ground
    peppercorns

Process the cheese, garlic, mayonnaise and sour cream in a food processor until smooth. Mix with the pepper in a bowl. Chill until serving time.

Makes 1 cup

Tomato Basil Dressing
Picola Restaurant/The Red Bar

3 cups olive oil
1 1/2 cups red wine vinegar
1/2 cup packed brown sugar
1/3 cup tomato paste
1 tablespoon Worcestershire sauce

3/4 cup chopped garlic
1 teaspoon basil
1/2 teaspoon oregano
2 egg yolks, or equivalent amount of
    egg yolk substitute

Mix the olive oil, vinegar, brown sugar, tomato paste, Worcestershire sauce, garlic, basil and oregano in a bowl. Process 1 egg yolk at high speed in a blender until frothy. Add half the olive oil mixture and process until smooth. Repeat the process with the remaining ingredients. Combine in a covered jar and mix well. Store in the refrigerator.

Makes 5 cups

SEAFOOD

Fish Tacos with Cabbage Slaw and Cilantro Aïoli

Cilantro Aïoli

1/3 cup chopped cilantro
green tops of 4 scallions, chopped
2 serrano chiles or jalapeño chiles,
    seeded and chopped
1 teaspoon drained capers

2 teaspoons minced garlic
1 egg
3/4 cup (or less) olive oil
salt and pepper to taste

Cabbage Slaw

2 cups finely shredded green cabbage
1/2 cup thinly sliced red bell pepper
1/3 cup thinly sliced red onion

1/4 cup thinly sliced basil
salt and pepper to taste

Tacos

1/3 cup olive oil
1 tablespoon fresh lime juice
1 tablespoon ancho chile powder
kosher salt and freshly ground pepper
    to taste

4 (4-ounce) fillets of halibut, grouper,
    amberjack or sea bass
4 (10-inch) flour or corn tortillas

To prepare the aïoli, combine the cilantro with the scallion tops, serrano chiles, capers and garlic in a food processor and pulse to mix. Add the egg and pulse until smooth. Drizzle in the olive oil very gradually, processing constantly until the mixture emulsifies. Spoon into a bowl and season with salt and pepper. Chill until serving time.

To prepare the slaw, combine the cabbage with the bell pepper, onion and basil in a bowl. Toss gently and season with salt and pepper. Chill until serving time.

To prepare the tacos, combine the olive oil, lime juice, chile powder, kosher salt and pepper in a small bowl. Brush generously on the fish fillets. Grill the fish until cooked through.

Grill the tortillas briefly until warm. Place 1 tortilla on each plate and top with the slaw and a fish fillet. Drizzle with the aïoli. Fold and roll the tortilla to enclose the filling. Serve immediately.

To avoid the possibility of salmonella from uncooked eggs, you can use an equivalent amount of egg substitute.

Serves 4

Grouper Beurre Blanc

Harry T's Boathouse

8 ounces grouper
2 ounces (71- to 90-count) shrimp
2 ounces crab meat
chopped parsley
1/8 teaspoon chopped garlic
1/8 teaspoon Harry T's Seasoning Blend

salt and pepper to taste
vegetable oil
1/2 cup white wine
2 teaspoons heavy cream
2 teaspoons butter
shaved almonds

Grill the grouper for 8 minutes or until done to taste. Sauté the shrimp and crab meat with the parsley, garlic, Seasoning Blend, salt and pepper in a small amount of oil in a skillet until cooked through. Add the wine, stirring to deglaze the skillet. Stir in the cream and reduce the heat. Stir in the butter.

Place the grouper on a serving plate and spoon the seafood beurre blanc over the top. Garnish with shaved almonds. Serve with rice pilaf and steamed vegetables.

Harry T's Seasoning Blend and other spices are available at the restaurant.

Serves 1 *or* 2

HERBED BUTTERS

Herbed butters are wonderful melted and served as a topping for fish. They can also be used as a spread for the bread served with the meal.

For Basil Butter, combine 1/2 cup softened butter with 1/2 cup chopped fresh basil, 1/4 cup grated Parmesan cheese, 2 tablespoons minced parsley and 1 teaspoon lemon juice in a bowl; beat until smooth. Chill, covered, until serving time.

For Sage Lemon Butter, melt 1/4 cup butter in a saucepan over medium heat. Add the juice and grated zest of 1 lemon, 1/2 teaspoon mace, 1/4 teaspoon rubbed sage and pepper to taste. Cook until bubbly and serve over fish.

Grouper Kiev

1/2 cup (1 stick) butter, softened
2 tablespoons chopped parsley
1 tablespoon lemon juice
1/4 teaspoon Worcestershire sauce
1/4 teaspoon Tabasco sauce
1 garlic clove, finely chopped
1/2 teaspoon salt

pepper to taste
2 pounds grouper fillets
2 eggs, beaten
2 tablespoons water
1/2 cup flour
3 cups bread crumbs
vegetable oil for deep-frying

Combine the butter, parsley, lemon juice, Worcestershire sauce, Tabasco sauce, garlic, salt and pepper in a bowl and mix until smooth. Shape into a log on waxed paper. Chill until firm.

Cut the fillets into 6 serving portions. Cut a horizontal slit in each portion with a sharp knife to form a pocket. Cut the butter into 6 equal portions and place 1 portion in each fish pocket; secure with wooden picks.

Beat the eggs with the water in a bowl. Roll the fish in the flour, dip into the egg mixture and coat with the bread crumbs. Chill in the refrigerator for 1 hour.

Heat oil to 375 degrees in a deep fryer. Deep-fry the fish for 2 to 3 minutes or until it flakes easily. Drain on paper towels. Discard the wooden picks.

Serves 6

Mediterranean Grouper

4 (6-ounce) grouper fillets or snapper
   fillets, rinsed and patted dry
1 teaspoon lemon pepper
3/4 cup chopped green bell pepper
3/4 cup chopped onion
1 cup sliced mushrooms
3 garlic cloves, crushed

1 teaspoon oregano
1/4 teaspoon salt
1 tablespoon olive oil
1/4 cup white wine
1 cup chopped plum tomatoes
1/3 cup (1 1/3 ounces) crumbled
   feta cheese

Arrange the fillets in a baking dish sprayed with nonstick cooking spray and sprinkle with the lemon pepper. Bake at 450 degrees for 10 minutes or until flaky.

Sauté the bell pepper, onion, mushrooms and garlic with the oregano and salt in the olive oil in a large skillet for 5 minutes or until the vegetables are tender-crisp.

Add the wine and cook for several minutes or until the wine is reduced by half. Add the tomatoes and reduce the heat to medium. Cook, covered, for several minutes or until the tomatoes are tender-crisp.

Remove the fish fillets to serving plates. Spoon the vegetable mixture over the fish and top with the cheese. Serve immediately.

Serves 4

HOW TO BLACKEN FISH INTENTIONALLY

Blackening fish is a technique that involves cooking at very high heat to achieve a spicy crust on the fish. Thin fillets of white fish, such as sole, grouper, tilapia, or tilefish, work best. For a Cajun spice mixture to use in blackening fish, combine 4 teaspoons hot paprika, 1 tablespoon garlic powder, 1 1/2 teaspoons onion powder, 1 1/2 teaspoons oregano, 1 1/2 teaspoons thyme, 1 tablespoon kosher salt, 1 1/2 teaspoons cayenne pepper and 1 1/2 teaspoons freshly ground black pepper in a shallow dish. Soak the fish fillets in milk in the refrigerator for 30 minutes. Shake off the excess and coat with the seasoning mix. Heat 2 tablespoons vegetable oil in a large skillet just until smoking. Add the fillets and fry for 2 minutes on each side or until cooked through.

Grouper Pecan
Flamingo Café

1 (12-ounce) can evaporated milk
2 tablespoons Dijon mustard
4 (6-ounce) grouper fillets

salt and pepper to taste
2 cups yellow cornmeal
olive oil

Roasted New Potatoes

1/4 cup olive oil
2 tablespoons dried thyme

salt and pepper to taste
8 new potatoes, cut into halves

Grilled Balsamic Vegetables

2 yellow squash, cut into 1/2-inch pieces
2 zucchini, cut into 1/2-inch pieces
1 yellow and 1 red bell pepper, cut into
   2-inch pieces

1 red onion, cut into 1-inch slices
2 tablespoons olive oil
1/2 cup white balsamic vinegar
2 tablespoons capers

Meunière Sauce

juice of 2 lemons
2 tablespoons heavy cream
1 tablespoon Worcestershire sauce

2 cups (4 sticks) butter, chopped
1/2 cup toasted pecans

To prepare the grouper, beat the evaporated milk with the Dijon mustard in a shallow dish. Sprinkle the fish lightly with salt and pepper and dip into the evaporated milk mixture. Coat with the cornmeal. Sauté in 1 inch of heated olive oil in an ovenproof skillet until golden brown on both sides. Place in a 350-degree oven to finish and keep warm.

   To prepare the potatoes, spread the olive oil evenly in a shallow baking pan and sprinkle with the thyme, salt and pepper. Place the potatoes cut side down in the pan and bake at 400 degrees for 10 minutes or until tender; keep warm.

   To prepare the grilled vegetables, toss the yellow squash, zucchini, bell peppers and onion with the olive oil in a bowl to coat. Grill just until tender. Combine with the balsamic vinegar and capers in a bowl and mix gently. Cover and let stand for 5 minutes to steam.

   To prepare the sauce, combine the lemon juice and cream in a nonreactive saucepan. Cook until thickened, stirring constantly. Stir in the Worcestershire sauce. Add the butter very gradually, mixing well after each addition. Stir in the pecans.

   Place the fish fillets on serving plates and top with the sauce. Add the potatoes and grilled vegetables and serve immediately.

Serves 4

Baked Snapper

1 onion, finely chopped	2 tablespoons chili sauce
1/4 cup chopped green bell pepper	salt and pepper to taste
2 cups chopped celery	1 (3- to 4-pound) snapper, head
1/2 cup (1 stick) butter	removed, cleaned
3 cups chopped canned tomatoes	3 cups corn bread dressing
1 tablespoon Worcestershire sauce	thinly sliced lemon

Sauté the onion, bell pepper and celery in the butter in a skillet until tender. Add the tomatoes and Worcestershire sauce and simmer for 30 minutes. Stir in the chili sauce and season with salt and pepper. Simmer for 10 minutes longer.

Season the snapper lightly inside and out with salt and pepper. Spoon the corn bread dressing into the cavity and place in a greased baking pan. Spoon any remaining dressing and the vegetable mixture around the fish.

Bake at 325 degrees for 1 to 1 1/2 hours or until the fish flakes easily, basting frequently. Remove to a serving plate and spoon the dressing and sauce around the fish. Garnish with lemon slices.

Serves 4

THE RED SNAPPER

Red snapper should not be confused with the unrelated rockfish that is erroneously marketed as snapper. The snapper, which is indigenous to Gulf Coast waters, is a vividly brilliant red fish with shimmering coloration on its head, back, fin, and tail, while rockfish is paler and has a bony face. The snapper's pure white flesh has a distinctively moist and delicate flavor. This fish will impress your guests, especially when served whole, and can be baked, broiled, grilled, oven-fried, or pan-fried. It is excellent served with seasoned butter.

Pan-Seared Four Peppercorn Tuna

Rutherfords 465

2 fluid ounces Cattleman's
   barbecue sauce
1 1/2 fluid ounces lager beer
2 teaspoons molasses
1 teaspoon cider vinegar
1/2 cup flour
1/4 cup cornstarch
2 teaspoons baking powder
3 ounces ice water
salt and white pepper to taste

3 asparagus spears
canola oil for deep-frying
1 cup peeled and julienned sweet potato
1/2 teaspoon cracked black peppercorns
1/2 teaspoon cracked green peppercorns
1/2 teaspoon cracked pink peppercorns
1/2 teaspoon cracked coriander
1/4 teaspoon kosher salt
1 (7-ounce) yellowfin tuna fillet
4 cups spring salad mix

Combine the barbecue sauce, beer, molasses and vinegar in a saucepan. Simmer over medium heat for 5 minutes; keep warm. Mix the flour, cornstarch and baking powder in a bowl. Add the ice water gradually, mixing well. Season with salt and white pepper. Coat the asparagus with the batter. Heat canola oil to 350 degrees in a deep fryer. Deep-fry the asparagus until golden brown. Deep-fry the sweet potatoes until crisp. Drain the vegetables.

    Mix the peppercorns, coriander and kosher salt together. Coat the tuna on both sides with the peppercorn mixture. Sear in a heated cast-iron skillet over high heat until done to taste. Spoon the sauce onto a serving plate and make a nest of salad mix in the center. Place the tuna on the salad mix and top with the fried sweet potatoes and asparagus.

Serves 1

Baked Wahoo

2 pounds wahoo fillets or other white
   fish fillets
lemon pepper and garlic powder
   to taste
2 onions, sliced
2 green bell peppers, sliced

2 cups sliced mushrooms
2 tomatoes, peeled and sliced
soy sauce and Worcestershire sauce
   to taste
1 cup (2 sticks) butter, chopped

Sprinkle both sides of the fish fillets with lemon pepper and garlic powder. Place in a baking dish. Layer the onions, bell peppers, mushrooms and tomatoes over the fish. Sprinkle again with lemon pepper and garlic powder. Drizzle with soy sauce and Worcestershire sauce.

Dot the layers with the butter and cover with foil. Bake at 275 degrees for 45 to 60 minutes or until the vegetables are tender and the fish flakes easily. Serve with French bread to dip in the cooking juices.

Serves 4

Clams Casino

Tony's Pasta by the Sea

18 middleneck clams
3/4 cup canned clam meat
1 cup finely chopped red bell pepper
1 cup finely chopped yellow onion
1 teaspoon chopped garlic
1 1/2 teaspoons mixed fresh herbs

1 tablespoon crumbled
   crisp-cooked bacon
1 teaspoon each salt and pepper
1 teaspoon olive oil
1/4 cup seasoned Italian bread crumbs

Shuck the clams, reserving the shells. Combine the fresh clam meat with the canned clam meat, bell pepper, onion, garlic, mixed herbs, bacon, salt and pepper in a bowl and mix well.

Oil the reserved clam shells lightly with the olive oil. Spoon the clam mixture into the shells and arrange in a baking dish. Sprinkle with the bread crumbs. Bake at 450 degrees for 10 minutes or until cooked through.

Serves 2 or 3

Crab Cakes with Mango Relish

Mango Relish

1 large mango, peeled and
   finely chopped
1/2 cup finely chopped red bell pepper
1/3 cup finely chopped red onion

1 tablespoon lime juice
2 teaspoons sugar
1/4 teaspoon salt
1/8 teaspoon ground red pepper

Crab Cakes

3 (1-ounce) slices white bread
1 pound lump crab meat, flaked
1/3 cup finely chopped onion
1/3 cup finely chopped cilantro
2 teaspoons peeled and chopped fresh
   lemon grass

2 teaspoons grated lemon zest
1/4 cup low-fat mayonnaise
2 tablespoons fresh lime juice
1 tablespoon fish sauce
1 egg white, lightly beaten
4 teaspoons peanut oil

To *prepare the relish*, combine the mango with the bell pepper, onion, lime juice, sugar, salt and red pepper in a bowl and mix well.

   To *prepare the crab cakes*, pulse the bread in a food processor 10 times or until coarsely crumbled; measure 1 1/2 cups. Combine with the crab meat, onion, cilantro, lemon grass and lemon zest in a large bowl. Add the mayonnaise, lime juice, fish sauce and egg white and mix well. Chill, covered, for 1 hour.

   Divide the crab mixture into 8 equal portions and shape each portion into a 1/2-inch-thick patty. Heat 2 teaspoons of the peanut oil in a large nonstick skillet over medium heat. Add 4 patties and sauté for 3 minutes on each side; remove to paper towels to drain. Repeat the process with the remaining peanut oil and patties.

   Serve the crab cakes with the mango relish. The relish is also good with any grilled mild white fish. You can find the lemon grass and fish sauce in Thai and Asian markets.

Serves 4

The photograph for this recipe appears on page 100.

Crab Meat Imperial

3 tablespoons butter
3 tablespoons flour
1 1/2 cups light cream
1/4 cup dry sherry
1 tablespoon lemon juice
1 tablespoon chopped parsley

1/2 teaspoon salt
2 tablespoon minced green bell pepper
3 tablespoons sliced green onions
2 tablespoons olive oil
1 pound fresh lump crab meat
1 cup buttered bread crumbs

Melt the butter in a saucepan and blend in the flour. Cook until bubbly. Add the cream and cook until thickened, stirring constantly. Stir in the sherry, lemon juice, parsley and salt. Cool to lukewarm. Sauté the bell pepper and green onions in the olive oil in a skillet until tender. Add to the cream sauce. Stir in the crab meat.

Spoon into individual baking shells or ramekins and top with the bread crumbs. Bake at 350 degrees for 15 to 20 minutes or until bubbly.

Serves 2 to 4

CRAB MEAT

Lump crab meat is preferred to claw meat for crab cakes. It is lighter in color and makes a more attractive presentation. Be sure to wash the crab meat in a colander, picking through it several times to remove all pieces of shell. Substitutions for crab meat include finely chopped shrimp or cooked white fish, such as haddock or whiting.

Crab and Shrimp Fettuccini

3 medium onions, chopped
3 ribs celery, chopped
2 green bell peppers, chopped
1 1/2 cups (3 sticks) butter
1/2 cup flour
3 cups half-and-half
16 ounces cream cheese, chopped
2 tablespoons chopped jalapeño chiles
3 garlic cloves, chopped

1/4 cup chopped parsley
2 pounds peeled cooked shrimp
1 pound crab meat
salt and Tabasco sauce to taste
16 ounces fettuccini, cooked and drained
1/2 cup (2 ounces) shredded
    Cheddar cheese
1/2 cup (2 ounces) grated
    Parmesan cheese

Sauté the onions, celery and bell peppers in the butter in a skillet until tender. Stir in the flour and cook for 10 minutes. Stir in the next 4 ingredients. Cook until the cream cheese melts and the mixture thickens, stirring constantly. Stir in the parsley, shrimp and crab meat. Cook over low heat for 20 minutes, stirring gently. Season with salt and Tabasco sauce. Add the fettuccini and toss to mix well. Spoon into a buttered 3-quart baking dish. Sprinkle with the Cheddar cheese and Parmesan cheese. Bake at 350 degrees until bubbly and the cheese melts.

Serves 8

Crawfish Jambalaya

1/2 cup chopped green bell pepper
1/2 cup chopped celery
3/4 cup chopped onion
2 garlic cloves, chopped
2 tablespoons chopped parsley
2 tablespoons vegetable oil
1 (10-ounce) can beef broth

1 1/4 cups water
1 (28-ounce) can tomatoes, chopped
1/2 teaspoon crushed thyme leaves
1/2 teaspoon chili powder
salt and pepper to taste
1 cup uncooked long grain rice
2 pounds peeled cooked crawfish

Sauté the bell pepper, celery, onion, garlic and parsley in the oil in a heavy saucepan until tender. Stir in the beef broth, water, undrained tomatoes, thyme and chili powder. Season with salt and pepper. Add the rice and mix well. Simmer, loosely covered, for 20 minutes or until the rice is tender. Add the crawfish and cook just until heated through.

Serves 6

Crawfish Fettuccini

1 pound crawfish tails
2 tablespoons butter
2 tablespoons minced shallots
1 tablespoon minced garlic
1 tablespoon Worcestershire sauce
2 tablespoons hot sauce, or to taste
2 cups heavy cream

16 ounces fettuccini, cooked al dente
salt and pepper to taste
1/4 cup chopped green onions
1/2 cup (2 ounces) grated
  Parmesan cheese
chopped chives and parsley
shaved Parmesan cheese

Sauté the crawfish tails in the butter in a large sauté pan for 2 minutes. Add the shallots and garlic and sauté for 1 minute. Stir in the Worcestershire sauce, hot sauce and cream. Bring to a boil and reduce the heat. Simmer for 8 minutes or until the sauce begins to thicken, stirring frequently.

Combine the crawfish mixture with the pasta in a large bowl and season with salt and pepper. Toss to mix well. Fold in the green onions and 1/2 cup Parmesan cheese. Garnish with chives, parsley and additional shaved Parmesan cheese. Serve with crusty bread.

Serves 4

Antilles Lobster Hash
Rutherfords 465

1/4 cup olive oil
1 cup finely chopped new potatoes
1/2 cup chopped purple onion
1 tablespoon chopped garlic
1 teaspoon jerk seasoning
1/2 cup chopped green bell pepper

1 Scotch bonnet chile or jalapeño chile,
  seeded and chopped
salt to taste
1 cup chopped cooked lobster meat
2 tablespoons chopped cilantro

Heat a large sauté pan over medium heat and add the olive oil and potatoes. Sauté for 3 to 4 minutes. Add the onion, garlic, jerk seasoning, bell pepper and chile. Sauté for 6 minutes or until the potatoes are tender but still firm. Season with salt. Stir in the lobster and cook just until heated through. Garnish with the cilantro. Serve with 2 poached eggs.

Serves 2

Oysters Bienville

½ cup (1 stick) butter
¼ cup flour
1½ cups milk
½ cup cream
1½ cups chicken broth
¼ cup white wine
1 pound cooked shrimp, peeled
  and chopped
1 (16-ounce) can mushrooms, drained
  and chopped

1 large onion, chopped
5 garlic cloves, chopped
4 dozen oysters on the half shell
rock salt
grated Parmesan cheese
bread crumbs
paprika to taste

Melt the butter in a saucepan and blend in the flour. Cook until bubbly, stirring frequently. Add the milk, cream, chicken broth and wine. Cook until thickened, stirring constantly. Add the shrimp, mushrooms, onion and garlic and simmer for 15 minutes.

Arrange the oysters in their shells on rock salt in a broiler pan. Broil for 2 minutes; drain the liquid. Spoon the shrimp mixture over the oysters and sprinkle with Parmesan cheese, bread crumbs and paprika. Broil just until bubbly and golden brown.

Serves 8

THE PEARL TO OPENING OYSTERS

Purchase ocean-area oysters during months that have an "r" in their name. First, make sure the oyster shells are scrubbed well under cold running water, then drained. Wearing gloves on both hands, place the oysters cupped side down on a firm surface. It is important to use a knife with a short, strong blade for opening oysters. Insert the point of the knife into the curved side opposite the oyster hinge and follow the bottom edge of the shell until the muscle is cut. Remove the top half of the shell and cut the oyster free. It can be served cooked or uncooked in the bottom shell.

Oyster Hash with Eggs

Hash Brown Potatoes

3/4 cup grated russet potatoes

2 tablespoons grated onion

1/8 teaspoon salt

pepper to taste

2 teaspoons butter

Hash

2 tablespoons butter

2 tablespoons vegetable oil

6 oysters, cut into 1/2-inch pieces

2 garlic cloves, crushed

1/2 cup chopped mushrooms

2 tablespoons chopped green onions

2 tablespoons chopped green
  bell pepper

5 eggs

3 tablespoons half-and-half

1 slice bacon, crisp-cooked
  and crumbled

To *prepare the potatoes*, combine them with the onion, salt and pepper in a bowl and toss to mix well. Melt half the butter in an ovenproof skillet over medium-high heat. Add the potato mixture to the skillet and press down with a large spatula. Reduce the heat to medium and cook for 7 to 8 minutes or until dark brown.

Invert the potatoes onto a plate. Melt the remaining butter in the skillet and slide the potatoes back into the skillet. Cook for 5 to 6 minutes or until the remaining side is brown. Keep warm in a warm oven.

To *prepare the hash*, melt the butter with the oil in a skillet. Add the oysters and garlic and sauté over medium heat until bubbly. Add the mushrooms, green onions and bell pepper. Sauté for 2 minutes.

Beat the eggs with the half-and-half in a bowl. Add to the skillet. Cook until soft-set, stirring frequently. Stir in the bacon. Place the potatoes on a serving plate. Spoon the oyster and egg mixture over the potatoes.

Serves 2

Scalloped Oysters

2 quarts shucked oysters
1/2 cup (1 stick) butter
2 1/2 stacks saltine crackers,
    coarsely crumbled

salt and pepper to taste
butter
1 1/2 cups milk
Tabasco sauce to taste

Drain the oysters, reserving 1/2 cup of the liquid. Melt 1/2 cup butter in a saucepan and add the cracker crumbs; mix well. Sprinkle 1/3 of the crumb mixture in a greased baking dish. Layer the oysters and remaining cracker crumbs 1/2 at a time in the prepared dish, sprinkling the oysters with salt and pepper. Dot with additional butter.

Combine the reserved oyster liquid with the milk, Tabasco sauce and pepper to taste in a bowl; mix well. Pour into the baking dish, just covering the layers. Bake at 425 degrees for 30 minutes.

Serves 6

Seared Scallops with Tropical Salsa

1/2 cup chopped pineapple
1/2 cup chopped mango
1/2 cup chopped cucumber
1/2 cup chopped red bell pepper
1 jalapeño chile, seeded and chopped

3 tablespoons chopped cilantro
4 teaspoons fresh lime juice
salt and pepper to taste
vegetable oil
1 to 1 1/2 pounds sea scallops

Combine the pineapple, mango, cucumber, bell pepper, jalapeño chile, cilantro, lime juice, salt and pepper in a bowl; mix well.

Heat a large skillet over medium-high heat and coat with a small amount of oil. Add half the scallops and sear for 2 minutes on each side or until golden brown, turning once. Remove to a serving plate and repeat with the remaining scallops.

Arrange the scallops on serving plates and serve with the salsa.

Serves 4

Orange Garlic Sea Scallops with Black Bean Sauce

Scallops and Marinade

1/4 cup olive oil
1/2 cup orange juice
1 tablespoon minced garlic

1 teaspoon grated orange zest
1 1/2 pounds sea scallops

Black Bean Sauce

1 teaspoon olive oil
3 slices bacon, chopped
1 small onion, chopped
1 tablespoon minced garlic
1 rib celery, chopped
1 carrot, chopped
2 jalapeño chiles or serrano chiles,
    seeded and minced

1 small red bell pepper, chopped
1 (15-ounce) can black beans
1 (15-ounce) can chicken stock
1/4 cup sherry vinegar
1/4 cup orange juice
1 tablespoon grated orange zest
1 teaspoon cumin
salt and pepper to taste

Assembly

cooked couscous or rice

grated orange zest

To marinate the scallops, mix the olive oil, orange juice, garlic and orange zest in a bowl. Add the scallops and toss to coat well. Marinate in the refrigerator for 30 minutes.

To prepare the sauce, heat the olive oil in a saucepan. Add the bacon and sauté over medium heat for 3 minutes. Add the onion and garlic and sauté for 2 minutes. Add the celery, carrot, jalapeño chiles and bell pepper. Sauté for 10 minutes or until the vegetables are tender. Stir in the beans, chicken stock, vinegar, orange juice, orange zest and cumin.

Bring to a boil and reduce the heat. Simmer for 10 to 15 minutes or until of the desired consistency. Remove from the heat and let stand for 5 minutes. Process the mixture in a blender. Return to the saucepan and season with salt and pepper. Keep warm.

To cook the scallops and assemble the dish, add them to a heated grill pan on the stove top. Cook for 3 to 4 minutes on each side or until cooked through. Spoon some of the bean sauce onto 4 warm serving plates. Spoon the couscous onto each plate and top with the scallops. Drizzle with the remaining bean sauce and garnish with orange zest.

Serves 4

The photograph for this recipe appears on page 100.

Royal Reds

Seasoned Rice

1/2 cup uncooked rice

3/4 cup water

1/4 teaspoon turmeric

4 garlic cloves, chopped

1 tablespoon chopped flat-leaf parsley

Shrimp

1 pound uncooked royal red shrimp

1/4 cup flour

6 garlic cloves, chopped

2 tablespoons butter

3 tablespoons dry white wine

To prepare the rice, combine it with the water in a saucepan and bring to a boil. Add the turmeric and reduce the heat to low. Stir in the garlic. Cook until the rice is tender. Stir in the parsley. Keep warm.

To prepare the shrimp, coat it lightly with the flour, shaking off the excess. Sauté the garlic lightly in the butter in a skillet over low heat. Add the shrimp and sauté just until golden brown. Stir in the wine. Simmer, covered, for 3 minutes. Turn off the heat and let stand for 8 minutes longer. Serve over the rice with crusty bread and a green salad.

Serves 2

Curried Shrimp and Rice

1/2 teaspoon vegetable oil

1 pound medium shrimp, peeled and deveined

1 1/2 teaspoons curry powder

1/2 cup chicken broth

1 (16-ounce) package frozen mixed broccoli, cauliflower and carrots

3/4 cup uncooked instant rice

1/4 teaspoon salt

Heat the oil in a large nonstick skillet. Add the shrimp and curry powder and stir-fry for 3 minutes. Remove the shrimp with a slotted spoon. Add the chicken broth and mixed vegetables to the skillet. Bring to a boil and cook for 1 minute. Stir in the rice and salt. Spoon the shrimp over the rice and remove from the heat. Let stand, covered, for 5 to 6 minutes or until the liquid is absorbed.

Serves 4

Greek Shrimp

1/4 cup (1/2 stick) butter, melted
12 jumbo shrimp or 24 large shrimp,
   peeled and deveined
1 egg
1/4 cup heavy cream
1/2 cup (2 ounces) crumbled feta cheese

3 or 4 drops of Tabasco sauce
juice of 1 lemon
1 large tomato, peeled and sliced
2 tablespoons chopped parsley
hot cooked rice

Spread the butter in a baking dish. Arrange the shrimp in a single layer in the dish. Whisk the egg and cream in a bowl until smooth. Add the cheese, Tabasco sauce and lemon juice and mix well. Pour over the shrimp. Top with the tomato. Bake at 400 degrees for 12 to 14 minutes or until bubbly. Sprinkle with the parsley and serve over rice. You can substitute strips or fillets of firm-fleshed fish for the shrimp if preferred, taking care not to overcook the fish.

Serves 4

Cajun Shrimp

1 teaspoon paprika
3/4 teaspoon thyme
3/4 teaspoon oregano
1/4 teaspoon garlic powder
1/4 teaspoon salt

1/4 to 1/2 teaspoon ground red pepper
1/4 teaspoon black pepper
1 1/2 pounds large shrimp, peeled
   and deveined
1 tablespoon vegetable oil

Combine the seasonings in a large sealable plastic bag. Add the shrimp and shake to coat well. Heat the oil in a large nonstick skillet over medium-high heat until hot. Add the shrimp. Sauté for 4 minutes or until cooked through.

Serves 4 to 6

Extraordinary Shrimp Pasta

2 tablespoons butter
1/2 red bell pepper, sliced lengthwise
1/4 cup chopped onion
1/4 cup chopped celery
1 garlic clove, chopped
1/2 tablespoon basil
1/2 tablespoon oregano
1 tablespoon fennel seeds
6 artichoke hearts, chopped
1/2 cup (4 ounces) sour cream
8 ounces uncooked peeled shrimp
8 ounces uncooked bow tie pasta
2 tablespoons olive oil
salt and pepper to taste

Melt the butter in a saucepan over medium heat. Add the bell pepper, onion, celery, garlic, basil, oregano and fennel seeds; sauté until the vegetables are tender. Add the artichoke hearts and reduce the heat. Simmer for 15 minutes. Stir in the sour cream and shrimp. Cook over medium heat for 10 minutes, stirring occasionally. Cook the pasta using the package directions and adding the olive oil; drain, but do not rinse. Spoon onto serving plates and top with the shrimp mixture. Season with salt and pepper.

Serves 8 to 10

Mexican Shrimp
Gourmet Entrées to Go

Red Chili Sauce

6 to 8 dried New Mexico chiles

1 cup chopped onion

1/2 cup vegetable oil

2 garlic cloves, minced

1/4 cup flour

4 cups chicken stock

cumin and salt to taste

Shrimp

1 pound medium shrimp, peeled

1 avocado, chopped into 1/4-inch pieces

4 cups cooked white rice

To *prepare the chili sauce*, remove the stems from the chiles and combine with water to just cover in a saucepan. Cook for 20 minutes or until tender. Process the mixture in a blender. Strain into a bowl and reserve the cooking liquid.

Sauté the onion in the oil in a 2-quart saucepan until tender. Add the garlic and sift in the flour, stirring to mix well. Cook until bubbly. Whisk in the chile liquid and chicken stock gradually. Simmer until slightly thickened, whisking constantly. Add cumin gradually, testing for the desired taste; season with salt.

To *prepare the shrimp*, warm 2 cups of the Red Chili Sauce in a skillet over medium heat. Add the shrimp and cook for 5 minutes or until the shrimp are cooked through. Stir in the avocado. Serve hot over hot cooked rice.

Store the unused Red Chili Sauce in the refrigerator or freezer.

Serves 3 or 4

Spicy Shrimp with Herbs

1/2 cup (1 stick) butter
1/4 cup olive oil
3 tablespoons lemon juice
2 teaspoons liquid crab boil
1/2 teaspoon Tabasco sauce
2 teaspoons paprika

1 tablespoon each chopped garlic,
    parsley, basil and oregano
3/4 teaspoon salt
1 teaspoon freshly ground pepper
1 pound unpeeled shrimp
cooked wild rice

Place the butter in a shallow baking pan and melt in a warm oven. Stir in the olive oil, lemon juice, crab boil, Tabasco sauce, paprika, garlic, parsley, basil, oregano, salt and pepper. Add the shrimp, stirring to coat well. Spread in a single layer. Bake at 400 degrees for 10 minutes or until cooked through; do not overcook. Serve over wild rice.

Serves 2

The photograph for this recipe appears on page 100.

Shrimp Scampi
Angler's Beachside Grill

1/2 cup (1 stick) butter
1 teaspoon lemon juice
1 teaspoon lime juice
1/2 teaspoon garlic-flavor oil
2 tablespoons wine
1/2 teaspoon Angler's Secret Spice
1 teaspoon Greek seasoning
8 large shrimp, deveined and butterflied

1/3 cup black olives
1 cup chopped tomatoes
1/4 cup chopped green onions
1/2 teaspoon Caribbean jerk seasoning
4 cups fresh spinach
11 ounces linguini, cooked and drained
chopped parsley

Melt the butter in a large skillet over medium heat. Stir in the lemon juice, lime juice, oil, wine, Secret Spice and Greek seasoning. Add the shrimp, olives, tomatoes, green onions and jerk seasoning; mix well. Cook until the shrimp turn dark pink. Add the spinach and mix lightly. Serve over the linguini and garnish with parsley.

    Angler's Secret Spice is available for sale at the restaurant.

Serves 1

Shrimp à la Jacques

Hollandaise Sauce

5 egg yolks

3 tablespoons lemon juice

1/4 teaspoon salt

cayenne pepper to taste

1/2 cup (1 stick) butter

1/2 cup white wine

Shrimp

6 tablespoons (3/4 stick) butter, softened

1 large garlic clove, minced

24 to 36 large shrimp, cooked, peeled
  and deveined

4 cups (16 ounces) shredded
  Gouda cheese

To *prepare the sauce*, combine the egg yolks, lemon juice, salt and cayenne pepper in a blender and process until smooth. Melt the butter in a saucepan and cook just until bubbly; do not brown. Add to the mixture in the blender very gradually, processing at high speed for 30 seconds or until the butter is incorporated and the mixture is smooth. Stir in the wine.

To *prepare the shrimp*, combine the butter and garlic in a small bowl and mix well. Place 4 to 6 shrimp in each of 6 individual baking dishes. Top with the sauce and a pat of the garlic butter; sprinkle with the cheese. Bake at 375 degrees for 2 to 3 minutes or until the shrimp are cooked through. Broil until light brown.

To avoid the possibility of salmonella from uncooked egg yolks, you can use an equivalent amount of egg yolk substitute.

Serves 6

Paella

4 to 5 cups chicken broth
1 1/2 teaspoons saffron, crushed
6 to 8 pieces chicken
1/4 cup olive oil
1 medium onion, chopped
3 garlic cloves, finely chopped
2 cups uncooked long grain rice
1 teaspoon salt
1/2 teaspoon pepper
1 pound chorizo, sliced

1 (16-ounce) can diced tomatoes
1 1/2 cups fresh or frozen green peas
1 (4-ounce) jar sliced pimentos
10 to 12 ounces lobster tail meat, cut
    into 2-inch pieces
1 1/2 pounds shrimp, peeled with the tail
    intact and deveined
24 mussels, scrubbed and debearded
24 clams, scrubbed

Bring 4 cups of the chicken broth to a boil in a saucepan. Stir in the saffron. Cut the chicken into 2-inch pieces. Brown in the olive oil in a large skillet. Remove to a bowl with a slotted spoon. Add the onion and garlic to the drippings in the skillet and sauté until the onion is tender but not brown.

Stir in the rice and sauté until the rice is translucent. Add the chicken broth, salt and pepper. Simmer, covered, over low heat for 10 minutes. Remove from the heat and stir in the sausage, tomatoes, peas and pimentos.

Place half the lobster, shrimp, mussels and clams in a large greased paella dish or baking dish. Spread the rice mixture over the seafood. Arrange the remaining seafood and the chicken over the top.

Bake, covered, at 325 degrees for 30 minutes; check occasionally to see if the remaining 1 cup chicken broth or water needs to be added. Remove the cover and bake for 10 minutes longer or until the rice is fluffy.

Serves 12

Scallops and Shrimp with Linguini

1 pound bay or sea scallops
1 pound shrimp, peeled
2 teaspoons chopped parsley
1 teaspoon (or more) basil
3/4 cup sliced green onions
3 garlic cloves, minced
3 tablespoons vegetable oil
2 cups fresh pea pods

1 small tomato, chopped
5 sun-dried tomatoes, chopped,
    or to taste
1/2 cup white wine
1/2 cup chicken broth
10 ounces linguini or angel hair
    pasta, cooked
grated Parmesan cheese

Mix the scallops, shrimp, parsley and basil in a bowl. Sauté the green onions and garlic in the oil in a skillet over medium heat. Add half the seafood mixture and sauté for 3 to 4 minutes or until the scallops are opaque and the shrimp turn pink. Remove to a bowl with a slotted spoon. Repeat with the remaining seafood mixture, adding it to the bowl.

Add the pea pods, tomato, sun-dried tomatoes, wine and chicken broth to the skillet and mix well. Cook for 2 minutes, stirring constantly. Return the seafood to the skillet and cook until heated through.

Spoon the pasta onto serving plates and top with the seafood. Garnish with cheese.

Sea scallops should be cut into halves before preparing this dish.

Serves 6

Cioppino

1 cup sliced onion
1/2 cup chopped celery
3 garlic cloves, minced
1 teaspoon olive oil
8 ounces white fish
8 ounces scallops
6 ounces crab meat
1 (6-ounce) can clams, drained
2 cups water

2 cups chopped potatoes
1 (28-ounce) can stewed tomatoes
1 tablespoon tomato paste
1/4 cup chopped parsley
1 teaspoon oregano
1 bay leaf
1/2 teaspoon pepper
2 tablespoons chopped parsley

Sauté the onion, celery and garlic in the olive oil in a saucepan until the onion is tender. Remove to a small bowl with a slotted spoon. Add the seafood and water to the saucepan. Bring to a boil and simmer until the fish flakes easily. Remove to a large bowl.

Return the onion mixture to the saucepan and add the potatoes, tomatoes, tomato paste, 1/4 cup parsley, the oregano, bay leaf and pepper. Bring to a boil and reduce the heat. Simmer for 15 minutes. Return the fish mixture to the saucepan. Cook, covered, for 5 minutes. Remove the bay leaf and sprinkle with 2 tablespoons parsley. Serve with hot crusty bread.

Serves 6

DESTIN FISHING RODEO

The Destin Fishing Rodeo takes place every October when the weather is perfect, with highs around 80 degrees and moderate sea breezes. Anglers aboard registered boats are free to compete for $100,000 in prize money. Destin, also known as the "World's Luckiest Fishing Village," has a long heritage as one of the premier places to go fishing. The name is credited to Captain Leonard Destin, who settled in the area in 1845 and pioneered the fishing industry. It is currently known as the billfishing capital of the northern Gulf of Mexico and boasts the largest charter boat fleet in Florida.

Royal Seafood Casserole

2 (10-ounce) cans cream of shrimp soup
1/2 cup mayonnaise
1/4 cup milk
1 cup chopped onion
1 (8-ounce) can sliced water
  chestnuts, drained
1/4 teaspoon nutmeg
1/4 teaspoon ground red pepper
1/4 teaspoon cayenne pepper
1/2 teaspoon salt

1/2 teaspoon seasoned salt
2 pounds scallops, sautéed and drained
2 pounds shrimp, cooked, peeled
  and deveined
1 1/2 cups chopped celery
3 tablespoons chopped parsley
2 cups rice, cooked and drained
slivered almonds, sautéed
paprika to taste

Mix the soup, mayonnaise, milk and onion in a large bowl. Stir in the water chestnuts, nutmeg, red pepper, cayenne pepper, salt, seasoned salt, scallops, shrimp, celery, parsley and rice. Spoon into a buttered shallow baking dish. Top with slivered almonds and sprinkle with paprika. Bake at 450 degrees for 30 to 40 minutes or until bubbly and heated through.

Serves 12

Seafood-Stuffed Peppers

1 1/2 pounds fresh shrimp
4 large green bell peppers
1 1/2 tablespoons butter
1 tablespoon flour
1 cup milk
1/2 cup (2 ounces) shredded
   Cheddar cheese
1 1/2 cups cooked long grain and
   wild rice mix

1 (1-pound) package frozen crab meat
   dressing, thawed
2 cups chopped celery
1 1/2 cups chopped onions
salt and pepper to taste
1/2 cup buttered fine bread crumbs

Cook the shrimp in enough water to cover until pink; drain, peel and chop into small pieces. Cut the bell peppers into halves lengthwise; discard the seeds and membranes.

Melt the butter in a saucepan and blend in the flour. Cook until bubbly. Stir in the milk. Cook until thickened, stirring constantly. Add the cheese and cook until the cheese melts, stirring frequently. Add additional milk if needed for the desired consistency.

Combine the rice, shrimp, crab meat dressing, celery and onions in a large mixing bowl; mix well. Season with salt and pepper. Add the cheese sauce and mix gently. Spoon into the bell peppers. Top with the buttered bread crumbs and arrange in a baking dish. Bake at 350 degrees for 45 minutes.

Serves 8

Seafood Tetrazzini

3 tablespoons butter
3 tablespoons flour
2 cups milk
1 cup light cream
1 teaspoon salt
1/2 teaspoon pepper
1 pound mushrooms, sliced
2 tablespoons butter

8 ounces thin spaghetti, cooked
  and drained
1 tablespoon melted butter
1/4 cup dry vermouth
1 cup cooked shrimp
1 cup flaked tuna
1 cup lump crab meat
1 cup buttered bread crumbs

Melt 3 tablespoons butter in a saucepan. Blend in the flour and cook until bubbly. Add the milk and cream. Cook until thickened, stirring constantly. Remove from the heat and add the salt and pepper. Cool to room temperature. Sauté the mushrooms in 2 tablespoons butter in a skillet until tender. Toss the spaghetti with 1 tablespoon melted butter in a large bowl. Add the mushrooms, cream sauce, wine, shrimp, tuna and crab meat; toss gently to mix. Spoon into a buttered baking dish and top with the buttered bread crumbs. Bake at 375 degrees until heated through and light brown.

Serves 6

Filet Mignon with Rum Glaze

2 dried ancho chiles
chicken broth
2 shallots, minced
2 garlic cloves, minced
3 tablespoons butter

¾ cup dark rum
3 cups chicken broth
2 tablespoons molasses
salt and freshly ground pepper to taste
4 (8-ounce) filets mignons

Pour boiling water over the ancho chiles in a bowl and soak for 1 hour; drain. Process the ancho chiles in a food processor until puréed, adding a small amount of chicken broth if needed for a smooth paste. Sauté the shallots and garlic in the butter in a saucepan over medium-high heat until tender-crisp. Add the rum and bring to a boil. Cook until reduced to ¼ cup. Add 3 cups chicken broth and bring to a boil. Reduce the heat to low. Whisk in the puréed ancho chiles, molasses, salt and pepper. Simmer until reduced to 2 cups.

Pour half the glaze into a bowl; keep the remaining glaze hot in the saucepan. Add the steaks to the glaze in the bowl, turning to coat well. Grill the steaks until done to taste, basting occasionally; discard the basting glaze. Remove the steaks to serving plates and sprinkle with salt and pepper. Drizzle with the hot glaze.

Serves 4

Filet Mignon with Spinach and Orzo
Four Winds International Food Market

½ cup olive salad
6 to 8 sun-dried tomatoes, chopped
10 to 12 garlic cloves, chopped
1 small onion, chopped
1 pound filet mignon, cubed

1 package fresh spinach
1 cup uncooked orzo
2 cups beef broth
salt and pepper to taste
crumbled feta cheese and lemon wedges

Combine the undrained olive salad, sun-dried tomatoes, garlic and onion in a saucepan and sauté for several minutes. Add the beef cubes and sauté until the beef is brown. Add the spinach and sauté until the spinach is wilted, tossing to mix well. Stir in the orzo and sauté for 2 to 3 minutes or until coated well. Stir in the beef broth and season with salt and pepper. Cook, covered, for 15 minutes or until the liquid is absorbed and the pasta is tender. Spoon into a serving dish and garnish with crumbled feta cheese and lemon wedges.

Serves 3 or 4

Pesto-Stuffed Ribeyes

Pesto

2 tablespoons pine nuts	3 tablespoons parsley
1 garlic clove	salt to taste
1/3 cup packed spinach	1/4 cup olive oil
1/2 cup packed basil	1/3 cup grated Parmesan cheese
2 tablespoons chopped oil-pack	1 tablespoon butter, softened
sun-dried tomatoes (optional)	

Ribeyes

6 (8-ounce) ribeyes, 1 1/4 inches thick	olive oil
1/3 cup grated Parmesan cheese	

To prepare the pesto, spread the pine nuts on a baking sheet. Toast at 325 degrees for 10 minutes, stirring several times and watching closely to prevent burning. Combine with the garlic, spinach, basil, sun-dried tomatoes, parsley and salt in a food processor; process until smooth. Add the olive oil gradually, processing constantly until well mixed. Add the cheese and butter and mix well.

   To prepare the ribeyes, cut a horizontal pocket in each steak, cutting to within 1/2 inch of the opposite side. Stir the cheese into 1/2 cup of the pesto. Spoon the mixture into the pockets in the steaks, leaving the edge unfilled to press closed. Drizzle the steaks with olive oil. Place the steaks on a hot grill and grill for 8 minutes. Turn and grill for 6 minutes longer for medium. Remove to a platter and cut into wide slices to serve. Store the unused pesto in the refrigerator for another use. You may substitute commercial pesto for the pesto in the recipe if preferred.

Serves 6

SOUTHWESTERN PESTO

Southwestern pesto is a unique pesto variation. It can be used to fill ribeye steaks or be served over pasta. Combine 2 cups cilantro leaves, 1 jalapeño chile, 1/4 cup pecans, 3 garlic cloves, 1/4 cup fresh lime juice, 1/2 cup freshly grated Parmesan cheese, 1/4 teaspoon salt and 1/4 teaspoon freshly ground pepper in a food processor. Process until chopped. Add 1/2 cup olive oil gradually, processing constantly until smooth. Store in the refrigerator or freezer until needed.

Martini Sirloins

3 tablespoons gin
2 teaspoons dry vermouth
2 tablespoons vegetable oil
4 garlic cloves, crushed
1/2 teaspoon basil

1/2 teaspoon rosemary
1/2 teaspoon salt
dash of angostura bitters
2 (10-ounce) sirloin steaks
pimento- or garlic-stuffed green olives

Combine the gin, vermouth, oil, garlic, basil, rosemary, salt and angostura bitters in a shallow dish for the marinade; mix well. Score the steaks in a grid pattern on both sides with a sharp knife, cutting about 1/8 inch deep. Add to the marinade and turn to coat well. Marinate in the refrigerator for 2 hours, turning several times.

Remove the steaks from the marinade, reserving the marinade. Place the steaks on a grill rack 3 inches from the heat source and grill for 4 to 6 minutes on each side or until done to taste, basting several times with the reserved marinade. Remove to a serving platter and garnish with olives on wooden picks.

Serves 2 to 4

Steak Kabobs

3 tablespoons soy sauce
2 tablespoons honey
2 garlic cloves, crushed
1 1/2 teaspoons grated lemon zest
1 teaspoon ground ginger

1/2 teaspoon red pepper flakes
12 ounces boneless sirloin steak
10 cherry tomatoes
6 large mushrooms
1 green bell pepper, cut into squares

Combine the soy sauce, honey, garlic, lemon zest, ginger and red pepper flakes in a bowl and mix well.

Cut the steak into cubes and place in a large sealable plastic bag. Add the marinade mixture and marinate in the refrigerator for 2 hours. Drain, discarding the marinade.

Thread the steak onto metal skewers, alternating with the tomatoes, mushrooms and bell pepper. Place in a broiler pan and broil until the steak is done to taste, turning 2 to 4 times. Serve immediately.

Serves 4

Lobster-Stuffed Beef Tenderloin

Beef Tenderloin

1 (6- to 7-pound) beef tenderloin
¼ cup (½ stick) butter, melted

4 or 5 cooked lobster tails
garlic salt and lemon pepper to taste

Wine Sauce

1 bunch green onions, chopped
½ cup (1 stick) butter

1 cup white wine

To *prepare the beef tenderloin*, split it lengthwise, cutting almost to the opposite side. Lay flat on a work surface and drizzle the cut sides with the butter. Arrange the lobster meat on the cut side and sprinkle with garlic salt and lemon pepper. Close the sides of the beef to enclose the lobster and tie in several places with kitchen twine.

Insert a meat thermometer into the thickest portion of the beef. Roast or grill until the meat thermometer registers the desired degree of doneness; keep warm.

To *prepare the sauce*, sauté the green onions in the butter in a skillet. Stir in the wine. Simmer for 5 minutes.

Place the tenderloin on a serving platter and cut into serving pieces. Drizzle with the sauce.

Serves 12

CLEANSE THE PALATE?

An intermezzo course is a refreshing interlude meant to cleanse the palate before an entrée is served. A light and fruity sorbet is often the choice. Combine a thawed 12-ounce can of frozen cran-raspberry juice concentrate, one 16-ounce can of cranberry sauce, ½ cup orange juice, ½ cup grapefruit juice and ½ cup lemon-lime soda in a blender. Process until smooth. Spoon into a 9×11-inch dish and cover with foil. Freeze until partially firm. Remove to a small bowl and beat until smooth. Freeze until serving time. Scoop into small bowls to serve and garnish as desired. Serve just before the main course.

Beefy Spinach Burritos

³/₄ cup chopped onion
1 teaspoon minced garlic
1 tablespoon olive oil
1 pound lean ground beef
1¹/₂ cups enchilada sauce
¹/₂ cup water
1 envelope taco seasoning mix
¹/₂ teaspoon salt

³/₄ cup packed coarsely chopped spinach
6 flour tortillas
1¹/₂ to 2 cups (6 to 8 ounces) shredded
    Monterey Jack cheese or
    mozzarella cheese
sour cream, sliced scallions, sliced black
    olives and salsa

Sauté the onion and garlic in the olive oil in a skillet over medium heat until tender. Add the ground beef. Sauté until brown and crumbly; drain. Stir in the enchilada sauce, water, taco seasoning mix and salt. Simmer, covered, for 5 minutes, stirring occasionally. Add the spinach and cook for 1 to 2 minutes or until the spinach wilts and the liquid evaporates.

Arrange the tortillas on a work surface. Spoon the ground beef mixture onto the tortillas and top each with 1 tablespoon of the cheese. Fold in the bottom edges of each tortilla 1 inch and roll the tortillas from the right edges to enclose the filling.

Arrange the burritos seam side down in a 9×13-inch baking dish sprayed with nonstick cooking spray. Sprinkle with the remaining cheese. Bake at 350 degrees for 15 minutes or until the cheese melts. Serve with sour cream, sliced scallions, sliced black olives and salsa.

Serves 6

SUPPER CLUB—OLÉ!

Supper clubs are very popular in the south and don't require that either you or your friends be gourmets. You just need to enjoy good food and each other's company. The club can meet monthly or at any chosen interval to prepare a predetermined meal. The hostess can prepare the entire dinner or just the entrée, or she can assign dishes for a potluck feast. For even more fun, you can have a unifying theme for the meal, the decorations, and the entertainment.

Blues Burgers

Barbecue Sauce

1/4 cup ketchup

1/4 cup packed brown sugar

2 tablespoons spicy brown mustard

2 tablespoons dark molasses

2 tablespoons cider vinegar

2 garlic cloves, minced

Mushroom Topping

8 ounces mushrooms, sliced

2 tablespoons minced onion

2 tablespoons minced shallots

2 tablespoons butter

2 tablespoons beer

salt and pepper to taste

Burgers

2 pounds ground beef

1/2 teaspoon cumin

1/2 teaspoon paprika

1/4 teaspoon chili powder

1/2 teaspoon salt

1/4 teaspoon black pepper

1/4 teaspoon cayenne pepper

1 cup (4 ounces) crumbled bleu cheese

4 onion rolls

To *prepare the sauce*, combine the ketchup, brown sugar, mustard, molasses, vinegar and garlic in a saucepan. Bring to a boil over medium-high heat, stirring to mix well. Reduce the heat and simmer for 30 minutes, stirring frequently.

To *prepare the topping*, sauté the mushrooms with the onion and shallots in the butter in a skillet. Add the beer and season with salt and pepper. Simmer for 15 to 20 minutes or until done to taste. Keep warm.

To *prepare the burgers*, mix the ground beef with the cumin, paprika, chili powder, salt, black pepper and cayenne pepper in a bowl. Shape into 8 thin patties. Place the bleu cheese in the centers of 4 of the patties. Top with the remaining patties and press the edges to seal in the cheese.

Brush the patties with the barbecue sauce and grill until cooked through, brushing occasionally with the sauce. Place the patties on the onion roll bottoms and spoon the mushroom topping over the patties; add the onion roll tops.

Serves 4

Three-Meat Loaf

Meat Loaf

4 slices white bread
1 carrot, coarsely chopped
1 rib celery, coarsely chopped
1/2 medium yellow onion,
   coarsely chopped
3 garlic cloves, crushed
1/2 cup loosely packed flat-leaf parsley
8 ounces ground beef
8 ounces ground pork

8 ounces ground veal
2 eggs, beaten
1/2 cup ketchup
1 teaspoon Tabasco sauce
2 teaspoons dry mustard
1/2 teaspoon chopped rosemary
2 teaspoons salt
1 teaspoon freshly ground pepper

Meat Loaf Topping

1/4 cup ketchup
2 tablespoons dark brown sugar
2 teaspoons dry mustard
1 tablespoon olive oil

1 small red onion, sliced into
   1/4-inch rings
3 tablespoons water
rosemary leaves (optional)

To *prepare the meat loaf,* trim the bread and process in a food processor for 10 seconds or until fine crumbs form. Remove to a bowl. Add the carrot, celery, onion, garlic and parsley to the food processor. Process for 30 seconds, scraping down the side of the container several times. Remove to the bowl with the bread crumbs. Add the ground beef, ground pork and ground veal to the vegetable mixture. Add the eggs, ketchup, Tabasco sauce, dry mustard, rosemary, salt and pepper. Knead until well mixed. Place a small piece of parchment in the center of a fine-mesh rack in a baking pan with sides. Shape the meat mixture into a loaf and place on the parchment.

To *prepare the topping,* combine the ketchup, brown sugar and dry mustard in a bowl; mix until smooth. Brush over the top of the meat loaf. Heat the olive oil in a skillet over high heat until smoking. Add the onion and sauté for 10 minutes or until golden brown. Add the water and cook until the water evaporates. Remove from the heat and cool slightly. Spoon over the meat loaf. Insert a meat thermometer into the thickest portion of the meat loaf.

Bake the meat loaf at 400 degrees for 30 minutes. Sprinkle with rosemary leaves. Bake for 25 minutes longer or to 160 degrees on the meat thermometer. Let stand for 15 minutes before serving.

Serves 6

Veal Chops with Red Wine Reduction

½ cup flour
⅛ teaspoon salt
1 tablespoon freshly ground pepper
8 veal chops
3 tablespoons olive oil
2 tablespoons brandy
1 garlic clove, crushed

⅔ cup red wine
2 tablespoons port
¾ cup beef broth
1 tablespoon red currant jelly
3 or 4 strips of lemon zest
¼ cup (½ stick) butter, chopped

Mix the flour with the salt and pepper. Coat the veal chops with the flour mixture. Heat a large skillet over medium-high heat and add the olive oil. Heat until hot. Add the chops and cook for 4 minutes on each side or until light brown and done to taste.

Drain the excess olive oil. Add the brandy to the skillet and ignite. Allow the flames to subside and remove the veal chops to a platter; keep warm.

Add the garlic to the skillet and sauté lightly. Add the wines, beef broth, jelly and lemon zest, stirring to deglaze the skillet. Cook until the liquid is reduced by ⅓ to ½. Remove from the heat and whisk in the butter. Discard the strips of lemon zest and serve the sauce over the veal chops.

Serves 4

LEFTOVERS ARE EVEN BETTER!

Some people say that leftover meat loaf sandwiches are even better the next day than the original meal! Remember that it is easier to slice the meat loaf when it has been chilled. Reheat the meat loaf slices and place each slice on toasted bread and add some tomato sauce or ketchup. There won't be any leftovers for very long!

Saltimbocca

1 pound top round veal
4 thin slices prosciutto
4 slices Monterey Jack cheese
$\frac{1}{2}$ teaspoon sage
flour

2 tablespoons olive oil
1 cup sliced mushrooms
2 teaspoons chopped shallots
1 cup dry white wine

Cut the veal into 4 pieces $\frac{1}{2}$ inch thick. Pound the veal $\frac{1}{8}$ inch thick with a meat mallet. Top each with a slice of prosciutto and a slice of cheese, trimming the slices to fit the veal. Sprinkle with the sage. Roll the veal to enclose the filling and secure the rolls with wooden picks.

Coat the rolls lightly with flour. Brown on all sides in the olive oil in a skillet. Add the mushrooms, shallots and wine. Cook, covered, over low heat for 10 minutes or until tender.

Remove the veal to a platter and keep warm. Cook the sauce in the skillet for 5 minutes longer or until reduced to the desired consistency. Serve over the veal rolls.

Serves 4

WHAT IS PROSCIUTTO?

Prosciutto is an Italian-style ham, a specialty of Parma, cured by dry-salting for one month and air-dried in cool curing sheds for six months or longer. It is usually cut into tissue-thin slices that highlight its intense flavor and deep pink color. Prosciutto di Parma imported from Italy is regarded as the best-quality prosciutto. You can find it at most quality butchers or meat counters in your market.

Rosemary-Skewered Lamb on Couscous with Curry Oil

Seagars

Curry Oil

2 cups olive oil

½ cup curry powder

Middle Eastern Couscous

2 gallons water
salt to taste
2 cups uncooked couscous
1 cup (4 ounces) chopped feta cheese

½ cup roasted garlic, about 4 whole
   garlic bulbs
1¾ cups chopped Italian flat-leaf parsley
pepper to taste

Lamb

3 to 4 pounds lamb loin
4 Roma tomatoes
1 red bell pepper
1 yellow bell pepper
1 red onion

16 cremini mushrooms
4 large rosemary skewers, soaked and
   drained, or 4 (12-inch) metal skewers
salt and pepper to taste
¼ cup chopped Italian flat-leaf parsley

To *prepare the oil*, heat the olive oil in a saucepan and stir in the curry powder. Remove from the heat and let stand until cool. Strain through a fine mesh or coffee filter into a squeeze bottle.

To *prepare the couscous*, combine the water with salt to taste in a large saucepan; bring to a boil. Add the couscous and cook for 8 to 10 minutes or until al dente. Rinse with water, drain and cool. Combine the couscous with the cheese, garlic and parsley in a bowl. Season with salt and pepper. Add ½ cup of the curry oil and mix well. Adjust the seasonings.

To *prepare the lamb*, cut it into 2-ounce cubes. Cut the tomatoes, bell peppers and onion into large cubes. Thread the lamb, chopped vegetables and mushrooms alternately on the rosemary skewers. Season with salt and pepper. Wrap the ends of the rosemary skewers with foil to prevent burning. Place the skewers on a heated oiled grill. Drizzle with some of the curry oil. Cook for 10 minutes for medium rare or until the lamb is done to taste.

Spoon the couscous onto serving plates. Top each serving with a rosemary skewer. Drizzle with curry oil and sprinkle with the parsley.

To roast the garlic for this recipe, cut garlic bulbs into halves horizontally and place on an oiled baking sheet. Roast at 350 degrees for 20 minutes or until golden brown and tender.

Serves 4

Fruit-Stuffed Pork Loin

1 (4-pound) boneless pork loin
1 cup dried cranberries
1 cup dried apricots
2 garlic cloves, cut into slivers
3 tablespoons chopped thyme

salt and pepper to taste
1/2 cup (1 stick) butter, softened
1 tablespoon molasses
1 cup madeira

Butterfly the pork loin, cutting to but not through the opposite side; lay flat on a work surface. Arrange the dried cranberries and apricots over the cut sides. Roll the pork to enclose the filling and tie with kitchen twine. Cut slits in the roll and place the garlic slivers in the slits. Rub the pork with the thyme, salt and pepper; spread generously with the butter.

Place the pork in a roasting pan. Whisk the molasses and wine together in a bowl and pour over the pork. Roast at 350 degrees for 1 1/2 hours or 20 minutes per pound, basting frequently. Remove from the oven and cover with foil; let stand for 15 to 20 minutes.

Serves 8

Thai-Style Pork Tenderloin

1 (2-pound) pork tenderloin
1 large red bell pepper, cut lengthwise
   into strips
3 garlic cloves, minced
1/4 cup teriyaki sauce
2 tablespoons rice vinegar or
   white wine vinegar

1 teaspoon crushed red pepper
1/3 cup creamy peanut butter
6 cups hot cooked basmati rice or
   jasmine rice
1/2 cup chopped green onions
1/3 cup chopped dry-roasted peanuts
8 lime wedges

Cut the pork tenderloin into 4 pieces. Combine with the bell pepper, garlic, teriyaki sauce, vinegar and red pepper in a slow cooker. Cook on Low for 8 hours. Remove the pork to a bowl with a slotted spoon and chop coarsely. Stir the peanut butter into the sauce in the slow cooker. Return the pork to the slow cooker and mix well. Combine the pork mixture with the rice in a large bowl and mix gently. Top each serving with green onions and peanuts. Serve with the lime wedges.

Serves 8

Crawfish-Stuffed Pork Chop
Rutherfords 465

Purple Potato Salad

³/4 cup cooked coarsely chopped peeled
    purple potatoes

2 ounces tasso, julienned

¹/4 cup julienned Vidalia onion

1¹/2 tablespoons Champagne vinegar

¹/4 cup olive oil

3 cups chopped arugula

salt and white pepper to taste

Red Pepper Coulis

2 teaspoons whole grain
    Creole mustard

¹/2 cup roasted red peppers

2 tablespoons garlic oil

Pork Chop

2 ounces crawfish tails, cooked, peeled
    and deveined

¹/4 cup finely chopped Vidalia onion

¹/4 cup finely chopped green
    bell pepper

¹/4 cup finely chopped red bell pepper

2 tablespoons (¹/2 ounce) grated
    Romano cheese

¹/4 cup panko bread crumbs

1 (12-ounce) center-cut bone-in
    pork chop

To prepare the potato salad, combine the potatoes, tasso, onion, vinegar and olive oil in a bowl; mix gently. Chill in the refrigerator for 12 hours. Add the arugula, salt and white pepper at serving time.

    To prepare the coulis, process the Creole mustard with the roasted red peppers in a blender or food processor until puréed. Add the garlic oil gradually, processing constantly until smooth.

    To prepare the pork chop, combine the crawfish tails, onion, bell peppers, cheese and bread crumbs in a bowl and mix well.

    Place the pork chop on a rack in a broiler pan. Broil at 550 degrees until seared on both sides. Set the oven to bake at 350 degrees. Cut a lengthwise pocket in the pork chop and stuff with the crawfish mixture. Place in a roasting pan and roast until cooked through.

    Spoon the potato salad onto a serving platter and drizzle the coulis around the salad. Top with the stuffed pork chop.

Serves 1 or 2

Pork Chops with Maple Pecan Sauce

4 (4-ounce) boneless center-cut
  pork loin chops
2 tablespoons flour
1/2 teaspoon ground ginger

2 teaspoons Dijon mustard
2 teaspoons vegetable oil
2 tablespoons maple syrup
2 tablespoons chopped toasted pecans

Place the pork chops between sheets of plastic wrap and pound 1/4 inch thick with a meat mallet. Mix the flour and ginger together. Spread the Dijon mustard on both sides of the pork chops; coat with the flour mixture.

Coat a large nonstick skillet with nonstick cooking spray and add the oil. Heat over medium heat until hot. Add the pork chops and cook for 3 minutes on each side or until brown.

Combine the maple syrup and pecans in a bowl. Add to the skillet, stirring to coat the pork chops well. Simmer, covered, for 4 minutes or until cooked through and tender, turning once.

Serves 4

Spanish Pork Chops

5 (1/2-inch) pork chops
2 tablespoons shortening
1/2 teaspoon chili powder
1 teaspoon salt
pepper to taste
3/4 cup uncooked long grain rice

1/2 cup chopped onion
1/4 cup chopped green bell pepper
1 (12-ounce) can tomatoes
5 green bell pepper rings
1/2 cup (2 ounces) shredded sharp
  Cheddar cheese

Brown the pork chops in the heated shortening in a skillet over low heat for 15 minutes; drain the skillet. Mix the chili powder, salt and pepper and sprinkle over the pork chops. Add the rice, onion, chopped bell pepper and undrained tomatoes.

Simmer, covered, over low heat for 35 minutes, stirring occasionally. Add the bell pepper rings and simmer for 5 minutes. Sprinkle with the cheese and simmer until the cheese melts.

Serves 5

Chicken and Wild Rice

1 stewing chicken
1 (4-ounce) can chopped black olives
2 (6-ounce) jars marinated artichoke hearts, drained and chopped
1 (8-ounce) can water chestnuts, drained and chopped
1 (4-ounce) can chopped mushrooms, drained

2 green onions with tops, chopped
salt to taste
6 cups cooked mixed long grain and wild rice
3/4 cup (or more) mayonnaise
1 cup (4 ounces) shredded white Cheddar cheese

Cook the chicken in enough water to cover in a saucepan until tender. Drain, cool and chop the chicken, discarding the skin and bones.

Combine the chicken with the black olives, artichoke hearts, water chestnuts, mushrooms and green onions in a large bowl. Season with salt and mix well. Add the cooked rice and mayonnaise; toss to mix.

Spoon into two 9×13-inch baking dishes and sprinkle with the cheese. Bake at 350 degrees until bubbly and heated through.

You may also prepare the dish in advance and chill for 1 hour or longer. Serve cold on a bed of lettuce. You may substitute chicken breasts for the whole chicken if preferred.

Serves 12 to 16

PASS THE CHEESE BREAD, PLEASE!

Cheese bread is an easy accompaniment to any main dish, but goes especially well with comfort food like Chicken and Wild Rice. Slice a loaf of French bread into halves horizontally. Combine 2 cups shredded Monterey Jack cheese, 2 cups shredded Cheddar cheese, 1/4 cup chopped onion, 1/4 cup chopped parsley, 1 cup mayonnaise, 1 tablespoon softened butter and 1/8 teaspoon garlic powder in a bowl and mix well. Spread over the cut sides of the bread and place on a baking sheet. Broil until the cheese is melted and bubbly.

Summer Grilled Chicken Wraps

2 large boneless skinless
   chicken breasts
salt and pepper to taste
juice of 2 limes
4 large flour tortillas
2 red bell peppers, julienned
2 small red onions, julienned

1 Anaheim chile, seeded and minced
3 cups shredded romaine
1/4 cup cilantro leaves
1/2 cup (2 ounces) crumbled goat cheese
3 tomatoes, coarsely chopped
juice of 1 lime

Sprinkle the chicken with salt and pepper and arrange in a shallow dish. Drizzle with the juice of 2 limes. Marinate in the refrigerator for 15 minutes. Remove the chicken to the grill, discarding the lime juice. Grill for 5 minutes on each side or until the juices run clear when the chicken is pierced. Remove to a cutting board and cool. Tear the cooled chicken into strips.

Warm the tortillas on the grill for 1 minute or until slightly puffed. Remove to a work surface. Layer the chicken, bell peppers, onions, Anaheim chile, lettuce, cilantro, cheese and tomatoes on the tortillas about 1/4 of the way up each tortilla.

Drizzle with the juice of 1 lime. Roll the tortillas to enclose the filling. Arrange seam side down on a serving platter.

Serves 4

FROM OUR FAMILY TO YOURS

Friends along the Emerald Coast support one another like family. There are neighborhoods where kids ride their bikes and parents host barbecues. From our family to yours—Enjoy!
The Pope Family—Kristen, William, and Ellie

Almond Lemon Chicken

Lemon Marinade

5 tablespoons lemon juice
3 tablespoons Dijon mustard
2 tablespoons vegetable oil

1 tablespoon chopped garlic
$1/4$ teaspoon white pepper

Chicken

4 boneless skinless chicken breasts
1 cup almonds
$1/2$ tablespoon vegetable oil
1 teaspoon cornstarch
1 tablespoon water

1 tablespoon vegetable oil
2 cups chicken broth
2 tablespoons orange marmalade
chopped parsley
hot cooked rice

To *prepare the marinade*, combine the lemon juice, Dijon mustard, oil, garlic and white pepper in a bowl and mix well.

To *prepare the chicken*, add it to the marinade and turn several times to coat well. Marinate in the refrigerator for 1 hour.

Sauté the almonds in $1/2$ tablespoon oil in a skillet until golden brown. Remove to a small bowl. Dissolve the cornstarch in the water in a bowl.

Drain the chicken, reserving the marinade. Brown the chicken in 1 tablespoon oil in a skillet for 6 to 10 minutes or until brown on both sides. Remove the chicken to a plate. Add the reserved marinade, the cornstarch mixture and the chicken broth to the skillet and mix well. Cook over medium heat until thickened, stirring occasionally.

Stir in the marmalade and cook over medium heat until bubbly. Return the chicken to the skillet and cook until heated through. Stir in the almonds. Garnish with parsley and serve over rice.

Serves 4

Bahama Bayou Chicken
Rutherfords 465

1 chicken
1/2 cup (1 stick) butter
1 cup chopped celery
2 cups chopped onions
1 cup chopped green bell pepper
2 tablespoons chopped garlic
1 teaspoon cardamom

1 teaspoon ground ginger
1/2 teaspoon turmeric
1/2 teaspoon dry mustard
1/2 cup flour
2 quarts chicken stock
2 chipotle peppers in adobo, chopped
1 (16-ounce) can diced tomatoes

Cut the chicken into 8 pieces. Brown the pieces on both sides in the butter in a large skillet; remove the chicken to a plate. Add the celery, onions, bell pepper, garlic, cardamom, ginger, turmeric and dry mustard to the skillet; mix well. Sauté for 3 to 4 minutes or until the vegetables are tender.

Add the flour and stir until well mixed. Cook until bubbly, stirring constantly. Stir in the chicken stock, chipotle peppers and tomatoes. Bring to a boil, whisking constantly. Reduce the heat and return the chicken to the skillet. Simmer, covered, over very low heat for 45 minutes to 2 hours, stirring occasionally. Serve with rice.

Serves 4

Chicken in Basil Cream

4 boneless skinless chicken breasts
1/4 cup milk
1/4 cup bread crumbs
3 tablespoons butter or margarine
1/2 cup chicken broth

1 cup heavy cream
1 (4-ounce) jar sliced pimentos, drained
1/2 cup (2 ounces) grated Parmesan cheese
1/4 cup minced fresh basil
1/8 teaspoon pepper

Dip the chicken in the milk and coat with the bread crumbs. Sauté in the butter in a skillet for 10 minutes or until the chicken is brown on both sides and the juices run clear. Remove to a plate and keep warm. Add the chicken broth to the skillet and bring to a boil over medium heat, stirring to deglaze the skillet. Stir in the cream and pimentos. Cook for 1 minute, stirring constantly. Reduce the heat and add the cheese, basil and pepper. Cook until heated through, stirring constantly. Spoon over the chicken.

Serves 4

Cilantro Chicken

1 chicken
1 cup chopped celery
1 teaspoon minced garlic
2 bunches cilantro
2 jalapeño chiles, seeded
2 poblano chiles, seeded

2 serrano chiles, seeded
1 green bell pepper, seeded
1 large onion, chopped
2 teaspoons minced garlic
1 tablespoon olive oil
salt and pepper to taste

Combine the chicken with the celery and 1 teaspoon garlic in enough water to cover in a large saucepan. Cook for 45 minutes or until the chicken is tender. Drain, reserving 2 cups of the cooking liquid. Chop the chicken, discarding the skin and bones.

Chop the cilantro, jalapeño chiles, poblano chiles, serrano chiles and bell pepper in a food processor. Sauté the onion and 2 teaspoons garlic in the olive oil in a large skillet. Add the chicken, reserved cooking liquid and chopped cilantro mixture. Simmer, covered, for 30 minutes. Season with salt and pepper. Basil maybe substituted for the cilantro.

Serves 8

Lemon and Herb Roasted Chicken

1 (3- to 5-pound) roasting chicken
1 large lemon, cut into 8 wedges
4 or 5 garlic cloves
2 tablespoons butter, softened

2 tablespoons extra-virgin olive oil
1/4 cup chopped parsley
1/4 cup chopped oregano

Place the chicken breast side up on a rack in a large roasting pan. Rub the chicken with the peel side of the lemon wedges and then place the wedges and garlic in the chicken cavity. Mix the butter, olive oil, parsley and oregano in a small bowl. Rub on the chicken.

Insert a meat thermometer into the thickest portion of the chicken's thigh, taking care not to touch the bone. Roast the chicken, uncovered, at 400 degrees until the meat thermometer registers 180 degrees and the juices run clear, basting frequently.

Serves 6 to 8

The photograph for this recipe appears on page 130.

Honey-Glazed Chicken

canola oil for frying
3 pounds chicken breasts and legs
1 cup buttermilk
2 tablespoons Morton's
   Nature's seasoning
1 tablespoon paprika
1 tablespoon salt

3 tablespoons pepper
1 cup flour
3 cups honey
1 tablespoon vanilla extract
1 tablespoon crushed red pepper
1 cinnamon stick

Pour enough canola oil to cover the chicken pieces into a deep skillet; heat to 360 degrees. Dip the chicken into the buttermilk and sprinkle with the Nature's seasoning, paprika, salt and pepper. Place in a plastic bag with the flour and shake to coat well; shake off the excess flour. Fry in the heated oil for 30 minutes or until golden brown and cooked through. Drain on paper towels. Mix the remaining ingredients in a saucepan or microwave-safe bowl. Heat or microwave to 120 degrees. Dip the chicken into the honey mixture and serve immediately.

Serves 4

Roquefort Chicken

4 boneless skinless chicken breasts
1 teaspoon cayenne pepper
3 tablespoons olive oil
5 garlic cloves, minced
2 cups sliced mushrooms
1 cup heavy cream

1/4 cup dry white wine
1 teaspoon herbes de Provence
freshly ground black pepper to taste
1 cup (4 ounces) crumbled
   Roquefort cheese
1/2 cup chopped flat-leaf parsley

Flatten the chicken to 1/2 inch thick with a meat mallet. Sprinkle with the cayenne pepper. Fry in the heated olive oil in a skillet for 8 minutes or until golden brown. Add the garlic, mushrooms, cream, wine, herbes de Provence and black pepper. Simmer, covered, for 20 minutes. Remove the chicken to an ovenproof platter and place in a warm oven. Boil the liquid remaining in the skillet for 5 minutes to reduce. Reduce the heat to medium-low and add the cheese. Cook until the cheese melts, stirring until the sauce is smooth. Spoon over the chicken and sprinkle with the parsley.

Serves 4

Chicken Enchiladas

4 large chicken breasts
chopped onion, celery and garlic
salt and pepper to taste
1 bunch green onions, chopped
3 cups shredded Monterey Jack cheese

3 cups shredded Cheddar cheese
2 cups (16 ounces) sour cream
2 (10-ounce) cans cream of chicken soup
1 (4-ounce) can chopped green chiles
12 (6-ounce) flour tortillas

Combine the chicken with onion, celery, garlic, salt and pepper in a saucepan. Add water to cover. Cook for 30 minutes or until the chicken is tender; drain. Cool and chop the chicken, discarding the skin and bones. Mix the green onions and cheeses in a bowl. Divide the mixture evenly into 2 bowls and set 1 bowl aside. Add the sour cream, soup and green chiles to the remaining bowl and mix well. Reserve 1 1/2 cups of the sour cream mixture. Add the chicken to the remaining sour cream mixture and toss to mix.

Spoon the filling onto the tortillas and roll to enclose the filling. Place seam side down in a baking pan sprayed with nonstick cooking spray. Top with the reserved 1 1/2 cups sour cream mixture and with the cheese mixture that was set aside. Chill, covered, in the refrigerator for 8 hours or longer. Bake, uncovered, at 350 degrees for 45 minutes.

Serves 8 to 10

Chicken Piccata

4 boneless skinless chicken breasts
salt and pepper to taste
1/2 cup flour
2 tablespoons each olive oil and butter
1/4 cup dry white wine

2 to 4 tablespoons fresh lemon juice
1 teaspoon minced garlic
2 to 4 tablespoons capers
1/4 cup (1/2 stick) butter, softened
2 tablespoons chopped parsley

Flatten the chicken to 1/2 inch thick with a meat mallet. Sprinkle with salt and pepper. Coat with the flour. Sauté the chicken in a mixture of the olive oil and 2 tablespoons butter in a skillet until golden brown on both sides. Remove to a platter and keep warm. Add the wine, lemon juice, garlic and capers to the skillet. Bring to a boil, stirring to deglaze the skillet. Reduce the heat and simmer for 5 minutes. Remove from the heat and whisk in 1/4 cup butter gradually. Stir in the parsley and spoon over the chicken. Serve immediately.

Serves 4

Italian Chicken Bundles

1 (10-ounce) package frozen chopped
    spinach, thawed and drained
1 cup ricotta cheese
1/2 cup (2 ounces) grated
    Parmesan cheese
1 teaspoon lemon juice
1/2 teaspoon garlic powder
1/2 teaspoon dried oregano
1/4 teaspoon ground nutmeg

3 medium boneless skinless
    chicken breasts, coarsely chopped
2 cups sliced green onions
1 tablespoon olive oil
salt and pepper to taste
8 to 10 egg roll wrappers
2 tablespoons margarine or
    butter, melted

Combine the spinach, ricotta cheese, Parmesan cheese, lemon juice, garlic powder, oregano and nutmeg in a large mixing bowl. Sauté the chicken and green onions in the olive oil in a large skillet over medium heat until the chicken is opaque and the onion is tender. Add to the spinach mixture and mix well. Season with salt and pepper.

    Grease eight 10-ounce custard cups or 10 large muffin cups and line each cup with an egg roll wrapper. Spoon the chicken mixture into the cups and fold the edges of the egg roll wrappers over the top. Brush with the margarine and press lightly to seal.

    Bake at 350 degrees for 20 to 25 minutes or until the tops are golden brown. Serve immediately.

Serves 8 to 10

MOVABLE FEAST

A progressive dinner involves three couples who get together and invite friends for an evening of good food. Each couple serves a portion of the meal in their home, and then the party moves on to the next couple's home. It is important to stick to a schedule and decide ahead of time how long guests should stay before moving on. For example, you can serve cocktails and hors d'oeuvre at the first home; salad and entrée at the second; and desserts and coffee at the third. This works out best if hosts live close enough together that guests don't have to drive between courses. What better way to remember the best of the Emerald Coast than a *Beach Appétit* movable feast!

Sun-Dried Tomato-Stuffed Chicken

½ cup pine nuts
½ cup chopped purple onion
1 tablespoon minced garlic
1 tablespoon olive oil
½ cup chopped oil-pack
  sun-dried tomatoes
¼ cup chopped kalamata olives
¾ cup (3 ounces) crumbled feta cheese

2 tablespoons (½ ounce) grated
  Parmesan cheese
½ teaspoon marjoram
½ teaspoon pepper
4 boneless skinless chicken breasts
1 tablespoon olive oil
coarsely ground pepper to taste

Sprinkle the pine nuts in a baking pan and toast at 325 degrees for 5 minutes or until golden brown, stirring several times. Increase the oven temperature to 400 degrees.

Sauté the onion and garlic in 1 tablespoon olive oil in a skillet until tender. Reduce the heat and add the sun-dried tomatoes, olives, feta cheese, Parmesan cheese, marjoram and ½ teaspoon pepper; mix well.

Cut pockets in the thickest portions of the chicken breasts. Spoon the sun-dried tomato mixture into the pockets; brush with 1 tablespoon olive oil and sprinkle with coarsely ground pepper to taste. Arrange the chicken in a baking pan. Bake, covered with foil, at 400 degrees for 30 minutes. Remove the foil and bake for 15 minutes longer or until cooked through and golden brown.

Serves 4

Red Pepper and Basil Chicken

Balsamic Marinade

1½ tablespoons balsamic vinegar

3 tablespoons fresh lemon juice

2 tablespoons extra-virgin olive oil

2 tablespoons chicken stock or broth

2 garlic cloves, minced

Chicken

4 boneless skinless chicken breasts

2 red bell peppers

salt and pepper to taste

10 basil leaves

To *prepare the marinade*, combine the balsamic vinegar, lemon juice, olive oil, chicken stock and garlic in a bowl and whisk until smooth. Reserve 3 tablespoons of the mixture for the sauce.

To *prepare the chicken*, add it to the marinade and marinate in the refrigerator for 20 minutes or longer; drain.

Grill the bell peppers over hot coals for 10 minutes or until evenly charred. Remove to a plastic bag and let steam for 10 minutes. Peel the peppers over a bowl, reserving the juice. Cut the peppers into ¼-inch strips and combine with the pepper juice and the reserved marinade. Season with salt and pepper.

Grill the chicken for 4 to 5 minutes on each side or until the juices run clear when the chicken is pierced with a fork. Remove to a platter and top with the pepper mixture. Garnish with the basil leaves.

Serves 4

BALSAMIC VINEGAR

Balsamic vinegar is considered the Champagne of vinegars. True balsamic is made in Italy from white Trebbiano grapes and adds an earthiness and fullness of flavor to dishes. It has both a sweet and pungent flavor at the same time. To make the vinegar, the juice of the grapes is cooked down and aged in barrels of either oak or cherry for a minimum of twelve years. When properly aged, it should have a dark syrupy consistency and be full in flavor. Of course, the longer the aging process, the more intense the flavor and the higher the price. When buying balsamic vinegar, look for Aceto Balsamico Tradizionale de Modena or Reggio; this is a true artisan-style vinegar and the best that one can purchase. It is best stored in a cool, dark place and used sparingly.

Chicken and Artichoke Casserole

1 pound boneless skinless
   chicken breasts
1 tablespoon margarine
salt and pepper to taste
1 (16-ounce) can water-pack artichoke
   hearts, drained and cut into halves
3 tablespoons margarine
1/4 cup flour

1/8 teaspoon nutmeg
2 cups chicken broth
1 cup (4 ounces) shredded
   Cheddar cheese
1/4 cup dry bread crumbs
1 teaspoon savory
1 teaspoon thyme
hot cooked rice or noodles

Cut the chicken into 2-inch cubes. Sauté in 1 tablespoon margarine in a skillet until opaque. Season with salt and pepper. Combine with the artichoke hearts in a greased 7×11-inch baking dish.

Melt 3 tablespoons margarine in a saucepan and blend in the flour and nutmeg. Cook until bubbly. Add the chicken broth gradually and bring to a boil, stirring constantly. Cook until thickened, stirring constantly. Add the cheese and cook until melted, stirring until smooth.

Pour the cheese sauce over the chicken and artichoke hearts. Mix the bread crumbs, savory and thyme together. Sprinkle over the top. Bake at 350 degrees for 25 to 35 minutes or until golden brown. Serve over rice or noodles.

Serves 4 to 6

Marinated Venison

Wine Marinade

2 medium onions, chopped

2 bay leaves

3½ cups dry red wine

2 tablespoons gin

8 black peppercorns, crushed

Venison

1½ pounds venison loin

salt and freshly ground pepper to taste

flour

¼ cup (½ stick) butter

3 tablespoons Cognac

1 cup Green Peppercorn Sauce
   (page 157)

1 shallot, finely chopped

¼ cup (½ stick) butter

8 ounces chanterelle mushrooms, or
   ¾ cup canned mushrooms

To prepare the marinade, combine the onions, bay leaves, wine, gin and peppercorns in a deep bowl; mix well.

To prepare the venison, add the loin to the marinade, coating well. Marinate in the refrigerator for 8 hours or longer, turning occasionally; drain the venison and pat dry. Cut the venison into twelve 2-ounce medallions. Pound the medallions to flatten slightly. Season with salt and pepper.

Dust the medallions lightly with flour, shaking off the excess. Heat ¼ cup butter in a large skillet over medium heat. Add the medallions and sauté for 3 to 4 minutes on each side or until brown on the outside and pink in the center.

Remove the medallions to a plate and keep warm. Add the Cognac to the skillet, stirring to deglaze the skillet. Add the Green Peppercorn Sauce and mix gently. Simmer for several minutes.

Sauté the shallot in ¼ cup butter in a small skillet until translucent. Add the mushrooms, salt and pepper. Sauté for 5 minutes. Add to the sauce in the skillet and mix well.

Place 3 venison medallions on each plate and top with the sauce. Serve immediately.

Serves 4

Green Peppercorn Sauce

Demi-Glace

4 cups beef consommé
1/2 cup red wine

1/4 cup tomato paste
2 tablespoons flour

Sauce

1/4 cup (1/2 stick) butter
3 shallots, chopped
1 sprig of fresh thyme, chopped, or
    1/4 teaspoon dried thyme
3 bay leaves
2 tablespoons vinegar-pack
    green peppercorns

1 tablespoon tomato paste
3/4 cup dry white wine
salt and freshly ground pepper
1/4 cup (1/2 stick) butter, chopped
1/2 cup Cognac
2 tablespoons vinegar-pack green
    peppercorns, drained

To *prepare the demi-glace*, combine the beef consommé, wine, tomato paste and flour in a saucepan and mix until smooth. Bring to a boil, stirring constantly. Cook for 20 minutes, stirring occasionally. Strain into a bowl.

To *prepare the sauce*, melt 1/4 cup butter in a large saucepan. Add the shallots, thyme, bay leaves and 2 tablespoons peppercorns with a small amount of the vinegar in which they were packed. Sauté for 3 to 5 minutes over medium heat. Stir in the tomato paste and cook for 2 minutes.

Stir in the demi-glace and wine and cook until the sauce thickens, stirring constantly. Season with salt and pepper. Strain into a bowl and return to the saucepan. Bring to a simmer. Whisk in 1/4 cup butter gradually. Stir in the Cognac and 2 tablespoons peppercorns.

Makes 6 cups

Cajun Fried Rice

1 teaspoon paprika
Cajun seasoning to taste
1 teaspoon kosher salt
½ teaspoon cayenne pepper
1 cup cubed uncooked chicken
1 cup sliced kielbasa or
    andouille sausage
1 tablespoon vegetable oil
8 ounces shrimp, peeled and deveined
1 tablespoon vegetable oil
½ cup chopped yellow onion
½ cup chopped celery

½ cup chopped green bell pepper
3 garlic cloves, minced
2 tablespoons chicken broth
2 tablespoons dry white wine
2 tablespoons fresh lemon juice
Tabasco sauce to taste
½ cup chopped Roma tomato
salt to taste
2 cups cooked white rice
¼ cup chopped scallions
¼ cup chopped parsley

Mix the paprika, Cajun seasoning, kosher salt and cayenne pepper in a bowl. Add the chicken and sausage and toss to coat well. Heat 1 tablespoon oil in a 14-inch skillet over high heat. Add the chicken and sausage and stir-fry for 5 minutes. Add the shrimp and stir-fry for 2 minutes. Remove the chicken, sausage and shrimp with a slotted spoon.

Add 1 tablespoon oil to the skillet and heat. Add the onion, celery, bell pepper and garlic. Stir-fry for 3 minutes. Add the chicken broth, wine, lemon juice and Tabasco sauce; stir to coat the vegetables well. Simmer until the liquid has nearly evaporated.

Stir in the tomato and return the chicken mixture to the skillet. Season with salt and mix well. Stir in the rice and scallions. Cook until the mixture is heated through and the shrimp is cooked through. Top with the parsley.

Serves 4

Jambalaya Pasta

1/2 pound hot bulk pork
    sausage, chopped
1/2 pound ham, chopped
2/3 cup chopped onion
2 ribs celery, chopped
3 green onions, chopped
1 pound chicken, cooked and chopped
3 (15-ounce) cans diced tomatoes
2 ounces tomato paste

2 bay leaves
Tabasco sauce to taste
thyme to taste
2 teasppoons salt
16 ounces fusilli or bow tie pasta,
    cooked and drained
2 tablespoons chopped parsley

Brown the sausage in a large heavy saucepan. Add the ham and sauté until brown. Add the onion, celery and green onions; sauté for 10 minutes or until the vegetables are tender.

Stir in the chicken, undrained tomatoes, tomato paste, bay leaves, Tabasco sauce, thyme and salt. Simmer over medium heat for 30 minutes, stirring occasionally. Stir in the pasta, adding water or chicken stock if necessary for the desired consistency. Cook until heated through. Discard the bay leaves and sprinkle with the parsley before serving.

Serves 8

MUSIC TO YOUR EARS?

Each year, the Northwest Florida Symphony Guild hosts its annual International Food and Wine Tasting. Usually held in February, this festival features the cuisine of more than twenty local participating restaurants and hundreds of different wine vintages. With the flavor of Mardi Gras in the air, this event is great fun for all.

Linguini with Pepperoncini and Bacon

8 ounces bacon, coarsely chopped
1 red onion, chopped
4 garlic cloves, minced
10 pepperoncini, drained, seeded
    and chopped

2 (15-ounce) cans diced tomatoes
salt and pepper to taste
12 ounces linguini, cooked
1/2 cup (2 ounces) freshly grated
    Parmesan cheese

Sauté the bacon in a large heavy saucepan over medium-high heat until crisp and brown. Remove with a slotted spoon to a paper towel to drain. Drain all but 3 tablespoons of the drippings from the saucepan.

Add the onion and garlic to the drippings and sauté over medium-high heat for 4 minutes. Add the pepperoncini and sauté for 1 minute. Stir in the undrained tomatoes and bacon. Simmer over medium heat for 2 minutes to blend the flavors. Season with salt and pepper. Reduce the heat to low and add the linguini, tossing to mix well. Cook until heated through. Sprinkle with the cheese.

Serves 4

Mushrooms and Prosciutto with Angel Hair Pasta

2 cups sliced mushrooms
2 tablespoons olive oil
1 teaspoon Emeril's Essence seasoning
1/2 cup chopped prosciutto
1/4 cup chopped green onions
1/4 cup chopped shallots

2 garlic cloves, minced
2 cups heavy cream
16 ounces angel hair pasta, cooked
    and drained
1/4 cup (1 ounce) grated Parmesan cheese

Toss the mushrooms with the olive oil and Emeril's seasoning in a bowl. Heat a skillet until very hot and add the mushroom mixture. Cook, covered, for 5 to 10 minutes or until the mushrooms are tender. Add the prosciutto, green onions, shallots and garlic. Sauté for several minutes.

Stir in the cream. Simmer until the sauce thickens slightly, stirring frequently. Add to the pasta in a bowl and toss to coat well. Sprinkle with the cheese.

Serves 8

Greek Spaghetti with Tomatoes and Feta

1 tablespoon olive oil
2 large garlic cloves, minced
1 teaspoon oregano
3½ cups chopped tomatoes
⅔ cup sliced green onions
3 tablespoons chopped parsley
2½ tablespoons lemon juice

4 cups hot cooked thin spaghetti
1 cup (4 ounces) crumbled feta cheese
5 tablespoons chopped parsley
freshly ground pepper to taste
1 boneless leg of lamb, cooked and
  sliced

Heat the olive oil in a large nonstick skillet over medium-high heat. Add the garlic and oregano and sauté for 30 seconds. Add the tomatoes, green onions, 3 tablespoons parsley and the lemon juice. Cook for 2 minutes or until heated through.

Combine the tomato mixture with the pasta and ¾ of the cheese in a serving bowl; toss to mix well. Sprinkle with the remaining cheese, 5 tablespoons parsley and pepper. Arrange the lamb in a fan pattern over the top and serve.

You may substitute sliced chicken breasts for the lamb.

Serves 4

GREEK HERITAGE

The Greek tradition is very rich in the area along Northwest Florida's Gulf Coast. One of the first pioneer families to this region was Greek. The family started a shipbuilding industry, which created many jobs and attracted even more Greeks from the old country. Ships from this family business were used locally in the fishing industry and farther south in the sponging industry.

As the Greek population grew in the area, so did the economy. Taxi services, banks, newspapers, theaters, and motels are among the many Greek-owned businesses that directly helped the area to prosper.

Today, Greek influence and tradition still thrive in our fast-paced life. This coastal area is still known for its fine fishing fleet and many restaurants that are Greek owned and operated. We are proud to include some of the Greek families' favorite recipes in this book.

VEGETABLES · SIDES

Char-grilled Artichokes

6 artichokes
olive oil

lemon juice
balsamic vinegar

Combine the artichokes with enough water to cover in a large saucepan and cook for 45 minutes; drain. Place on a heated grill and brush with olive oil. Grill until the tips of the leaves begin to char.

Drizzle with lemon juice and grill for 3 to 4 minutes longer or until tender. Serve with a mixture of olive oil and balsamic vinegar.

Serves 6

Asparagus Pastry Bundles

8 long thin slices prosciutto
16 asparagus spears, trimmed
1 sheet frozen puff pastry, thawed

1 egg, beaten
Hollandaise Sauce (optional, below)

Cut the prosciutto slices into halves lengthwise. Wrap 1 half around each asparagus spear, leaving the tip exposed. Cut the pastry sheet into 4 rectangles. Arrange 4 wrapped asparagus spears diagonally across each pastry rectangle. Fold the pastry over the bottoms of the spears, then over the sides, leaving the tips exposed.

Brush the bundles with the egg. Arrange on a baking sheet. Bake at 350 degrees for 15 minutes or until puffed and golden brown. Top with Hollandaise Sauce if desired.

Serves 4

HOLLANDAISE SAUCE

Divide ½ cup softened butter into 3 portions. Combine 1 portion of the butter with 4 beaten egg yolks in a double boiler. Bring the water in the double boiler to a boil and reduce the heat to low. Cook until the butter melts, stirring constantly. Add the remaining portions of butter 1 at a time and cook until melted after each addition, stirring constantly. Remove the top portion of the double boiler from the heat and stir the sauce for 2 minutes. Stir in 2 tablespoons lemon juice 1 teaspoon at a time. Stir in ½ teaspoon salt. Place back over the simmering water and cook for 2 to 3 minutes or until smooth and thick, stirring constantly. Remove from the heat and serve immediately over vegetables or chicken.

Roasted Asparagus

30 asparagus spears
¼ teaspoon salt
⅛ teaspoon pepper
2 tablespoons butter

1 tablespoon soy sauce
1½ teaspoons balsamic vinegar
¾ cup (3 ounces) shaved Parmesan
    cheese curls

Arrange the asparagus spears in a single layer on a baking sheet oiled with olive oil. Sprinkle with the salt and pepper. Roast at 400 degrees for 12 minutes or until tender. Remove to a serving platter and keep warm.

    Melt the butter in a small skillet over medium heat. Cook for 3 minutes or until the butter is light brown, shaking the skillet occasionally. Remove from the heat and stir in the soy sauce and balsamic vinegar. Drizzle over the asparagus and top with the cheese. Serve immediately.

Serves 6

Chilled Mediterranean Beans

1 pound fresh green beans, broken
    into 1 1/2-inch pieces
1 teaspoon salt
1/4 cup olive oil
2 garlic cloves, minced
2 tablespoons red wine vinegar
1/2 cup kalamata olives,
    coarsely chopped

1/2 cup green Spanish olives,
    coarsely chopped
1 teaspoon oregano
1 teaspoon salt
1/4 teaspoon freshly ground pepper
1 large tomato, seeded and chopped
1 cup (4 ounces) crumbled feta cheese

Bring enough water to cover the beans to a boil in a saucepan. Add the beans and
1 teaspoon salt. Cook for 6 to 8 minutes or until tender-crisp. Drain the beans and plunge
into ice water to stop the cooking process. Drain again and remove to a serving dish.

Heat the olive oil in a small skillet. Add the garlic and sauté for 30 seconds or until
fragrant. Remove from the heat and stir in the vinegar, olives, oregano, 1 teaspoon salt
and the pepper. Pour over the beans and toss to coat well.

Chill the beans for 3 hours or longer. Add the tomato at serving time and toss lightly.
Sprinkle with the cheese.

Serves 4 to 6

Green Beans with Pine Nuts

1 pound fresh green beans, trimmed
1/4 cup olive oil
1/3 cup toasted pine nuts
1/4 cup red wine vinegar
2 garlic cloves, minced
1 teaspoon chopped fresh cilantro

1 teaspoon chopped fresh oregano, or
    1/2 teaspoon dried oregano
salt and pepper to taste
1/4 cup (1 ounce) grated
    Parmesan cheese

Combine the green beans with enough water to cover in a saucepan. Cook just until
tender; drain and rinse with cold water. Heat the olive oil in a large skillet and stir in the
pine nuts, vinegar, garlic, cilantro and oregano. Add the green beans and cook over
medium heat until heated through. Sprinkle with salt and pepper. Top with the cheese.

Serves 2

Broccoli and Roasted Mushrooms

Balsamic Mustard Sauce

2 tablespoons coarse-grain mustard

3 tablespoons balsamic vinegar

1 tablespoon chopped parsley

$1/2$ teaspoon oregano

freshly ground pepper to taste

3 tablespoons olive oil

Broccoli and Mushrooms

2 pounds mushrooms

5 shallots, chopped

$1/3$ cup lemon juice

1 tablespoon olive oil

2 tablespoons chopped parsley

1 teaspoon thyme

$1/2$ teaspoon salt

$1/4$ teaspoon pepper

$2 1/2$ pounds broccoli florets

red leaf lettuce

To *prepare the sauce*, combine the mustard, balsamic vinegar, parsley, oregano and pepper in a small bowl and whisk until smooth. Add the olive oil in a fine stream, whisking constantly until combined.

To *prepare the vegetables*, combine the mushrooms, shallots, lemon juice, olive oil, parsley, thyme, salt and pepper in a large bowl and toss to coat well. Spread in a single layer in a large baking dish. Roast at 450 degrees for 20 to 25 minutes or until tender. Remove to a bowl and keep warm.

Steam the broccoli florets over boiling water for 4 minutes or until tender-crisp; drain. Add to the mushroom mixture. Add the sauce and toss lightly to mix well. Serve on a bed of lettuce.

Serves 8

The photograph for this recipe appears on page 162.

Baked Cinnamon Carrots

2 cups coarsely mashed cooked carrots,
    about 8 large carrots
1 cup sugar

3 tablespoons flour
1/2 cup (1 stick) butter, melted
1 1/2 tablespoons cinnamon

Combine the carrots, sugar, flour, butter and cinnamon in a bowl and mix well. Spoon into a greased small baking dish; the mixture should be at least 2 inches deep in the dish. Bake at 400 degrees for 15 minutes. Reduce the oven temperature to 350 degrees and bake for 45 minutes longer.

You can substitute 2 cans of cooked sliced carrots for the mashed fresh carrots if preferred.

Serves 4

Choctaw Corn Pudding

6 ears of fresh corn, or 2 (12-ounce)
    cans whole kernel corn, drained
6 tablespoons (3/4 stick) butter
2 tablespoons sugar
2 tablespoons flour
1/2 cup light cream

4 eggs, beaten
1 1/2 teaspoons baking powder
2 tablespoons butter, melted
2 tablespoons brown sugar
1/4 teaspoon cinnamon

Cut the kernels from the corn cobs. Melt 6 tablespoons butter with the sugar in a small saucepan. Stir in the flour and remove from the heat. Stir in the cream gradually. Add the eggs and baking powder and mix well. Stir in the corn.

Spoon the mixture into a buttered 1 1/2-quart baking dish. Bake at 350 degrees for 40 minutes or until a knife inserted into the center comes out clean. Drizzle with 2 tablespoons melted butter.

Mix the brown sugar and cinnamon together and sprinkle over the corn mixture. Bake for 5 to 7 minutes longer or until golden brown.

Serves 6 to 8

Summer Corn-off-the-Cob

4 ears of fresh white corn
2 tablespoons unsalted butter
5 large shallots, chopped
sugar to taste

1/4 teaspoon salt
1/8 teaspoon freshly ground pepper
3 tablespoons chopped thyme

Cut the kernels from the corn cobs and measure 3 cups. Melt the butter in a large skillet over medium heat. Add the corn, shallots, sugar, salt and pepper and mix well. Cook for 5 minutes, stirring occasionally. Stir in the thyme and cook for 5 minutes longer. Adjust the seasonings and serve immediately.

Serves 4

The photograph for this recipe appears on page 162.

Burgundy Mushrooms

2 cups water
3 beef bouillon cubes
3 chicken bouillon cubes
4 cups burgundy
1 1/2 cups (3 sticks) butter
2 tablespoons Worcestershire sauce

1 teaspoon dillseeds
1 teaspoon garlic powder
1 teaspoon pepper
4 pounds mushrooms
salt to taste

Bring the water to a boil in a large heavy saucepan. Add the bouillon cubes and stir to dissolve completely. Add the wine, butter, Worcestershire sauce, dillseeds, garlic powder and pepper; return to a boil. Add the mushrooms and reduce the heat. Simmer, covered, for 5 hours. Simmer, uncovered, for 4 hours longer or until the liquid is reduced enough to just cover the mushrooms. Season to taste with salt. Serve hot with grilled steaks.

Serves 12 to 16

Creamy Mushrooms in Pastry Shells

2 refrigerator pie pastries
1/4 cup (1/2 stick) butter
1/4 cup flour
1 teaspoon salt
1 cup light cream
1 cup milk

3 (8-ounce) cans mushroom
   pieces, drained
2 to 3 tablespoons grated onion
1 tablespoon Worcestershire sauce
1 teaspoon pepper

Cut circles from the pie pastry large enough to cover small muffin cups in inverted muffin pans. Mold the circles over the muffin cups. Bake at 350 degrees until golden brown. Remove to a wire rack to cool.

Melt the butter in a double boiler and blend in the flour and salt. Cook until bubbly, stirring constantly. Add the cream and milk. Cook until thickened and smooth, stirring constantly. Stir in the mushrooms, onion, Worcestershire sauce and pepper. Cook until heated through. Spoon into the pastry shells to serve.

You can keep the mushroom mixture warm in the double boiler for up to 1 hour.

Serves 6

Spicy Okra

1 pound fresh okra, 3 inches or
   less in length
1 tablespoon olive oil

3 tablespoons minced garlic
1/2 teaspoon crushed red pepper flakes
salt and black pepper to taste

Trim just the tops of the okra pods, leaving the stems intact. Heat the olive oil in a large skillet until medium-hot but not smoking. Add the okra and sauté for 45 seconds, stirring frequently. Add the garlic, red pepper flakes, salt and black pepper. Sauté for 1 minute longer. Serve immediately.

Serves 3

The photograph for this recipe appears on page 162.

Vidalia Onion Casserole

2 tablespoons butter or margarine
2 tablespoons flour
1 cup chicken broth
1 cup water
1 (5-ounce) can evaporated milk
3 cups Vidalia onion wedges

1/2 cup slivered almonds
1/2 teaspoon salt
1/2 teaspoon pepper
1 cup bread crumbs
1/2 cup (2 ounces) shredded
   Cheddar cheese

Melt the butter in a saucepan. Stir in the flour and cook until bubbly. Add the chicken broth, water and evaporated milk. Cook until thickened, stirring constantly. Add the onions, almonds, salt and pepper; mix well.

Spoon into a buttered 1 1/2-quart baking dish. Top with the bread crumbs and cheese. Bake at 375 degrees for 30 minutes or until set.

Serves 6

VIDALIA ONIONS

If you live in the south, you know that Vidalia onions are among the sweetest and best-tasting onions. Mose Coleman was the Georgia farmer who discovered that his onions were sweet enough to eat like fruit. The onion is higher in water and sugar content, which makes it mild in flavor and highly desired. Vidalia onions are grown exclusively in a 20-county area in Georgia, and part of their flavor comes from the soil, which lacks sulfur. This is important, because onions planted in different soils will have different flavors. They are best served raw to appreciate their flavor, so use them in any recipe that calls for uncooked onion, but they are delicious cooked as well. June is the month for harvesting Vidalia onions, so you will have to wait for summer to try the Vidalia Onion Casserole, and we do not recommend substituting any other onion for the Vidalias in this dish.

Crisp Rosemary Potatoes

1 tablespoon extra-virgin olive oil
salt and freshly ground pepper to taste
2 pounds small Yukon Gold potatoes,
    cut into halves

3 tablespoons extra-virgin olive oil
4 garlic cloves, thinly sliced
2 tablespoons chopped fresh rosemary

Brush a baking sheet with 1 tablespoon olive oil and sprinkle with salt and pepper. Arrange the potatoes cut side down on the baking sheet. Bake at 400 degrees for 45 minutes or until crisp and golden brown. Remove to a bowl.

Heat 3 tablespoons olive oil in a large skillet over medium-low heat. Add the garlic and rosemary. Sauté just until crisp and light brown; do not overbrown the garlic or it will become bitter. Pour over the potatoes and toss to coat well. Adjust the salt and pepper.

Serves 8

Sweet Potatoes Anna

3 large sweet potatoes
1/2 cup (1 stick) butter, melted
salt, pepper and nutmeg to taste
cayenne pepper to taste (optional)

1/2 cup (2 ounces) grated aged
    Parmesan cheese
1/4 cup (2 ounces) sour cream
1 tablespoon chopped fresh chives

Cut the sweet potatoes into thin slices with a food processor or mandoline, placing them in a bowl of ice water as they are sliced to prevent discoloration. Dry each slice well and dip into the melted butter.

Arrange some of the slices in an overlapping circular pattern to cover the bottoms of 6 greased custard cups. Sprinkle lightly with salt and pepper. Add a second layer in each cup, reversing the direction of the layer. Sprinkle with nutmeg, cayenne pepper and Parmesan cheese. Continue to reverse the direction of the sweet potato layers, sprinkling alternate layers as above, until the cups are filled.

Place on a baking sheet. Bake, covered with foil, at 425 degrees for 20 minutes. Remove the foil and bake for 15 minutes or until the tops are brown and crusty. Tip each custard cup to drain any excess butter. Invert onto a serving plate. Garnish with the sour cream and chives.

Serves 6

Fresh Tomato Pie

2 cups (8 ounces) shredded
   mozzarella cheese
1 unbaked (9-inch) pie shell
2 tablespoons chopped basil

4 tomatoes, sliced
1/2 teaspoon salt
1/4 teaspoon pepper
1 tablespoon olive oil

Spread the cheese in the pie shell and sprinkle with the basil. Arrange the tomato slices as evenly as possible in the prepared pie shell. Sprinkle with the salt and pepper and drizzle with the olive oil. Bake at 400 degrees for 30 to 40 minutes or until the crust is golden brown. Cut into wedges to serve.

Serves 6

Greek-Style Zucchini

4 (6-inch) zucchini
2 tablespoons butter, melted
1/4 teaspoon dill weed

freshly ground pepper to taste
4 to 5 tablespoons (1 ounce or more)
   crumbled feta cheese

Slice the zucchini 1/2 inch thick. Toss with the melted butter, dill weed and pepper in a bowl, coating well. Spread on a baking sheet lightly sprayed with nonstick cooking spray. Cover tightly with foil.

Bake at 350 degrees for 20 minutes or until tender-crisp; bake for 10 minutes longer for tender. Combine with the cheese in a bowl and toss gently to mix.

Serves 4

Caramelized Vegetables

1 pound Yukon Gold potatoes
2 large carrots
2 zucchini
2 yellow squash
1 Japanese eggplant, or
   1/2 American eggplant
1 large red onion

1 fennel bulb
1/4 cup extra-virgin olive oil
1 pound asparagus, trimmed
1 tablespoon fennel seeds, crushed
   or ground
salt to taste
1 tablespoon extra-virgin olive oil

Cut the unpeeled potatoes into 1-inch pieces. Peel the carrots and cut into 1/2-inch pieces. Trim the zucchini, yellow squash and eggplant and slice lengthwise; then slice into 1/2-inch pieces. Cut the onion and fennel bulb into 1/2-inch wedges.

Combine the potatoes with enough salted water to cover in a large saucepan. Bring to a boil and reduce the heat. Simmer for 7 minutes. Add the carrots and simmer for 1 minute; drain and place in a bowl.

Heat a very large ovenproof skillet over high heat. Add 1/4 cup olive oil and heat until hot. Add the potatoes and carrots. Sauté for 1 minute. Add the onion. Cook for 10 minutes or until the vegetables are brown, stirring occasionally; reduce the heat if necessary to prevent overbrowning.

Add the fennel bulb, zucchini, yellow squash, eggplant, asparagus, fennel seeds and salt to taste; toss to mix well. Drizzle with 1 tablespoon olive oil and toss again. Roast at 425 degrees for 20 to 25 minutes or until the vegetables are caramelized a deep brown, stirring occasionally. Serve hot.

Serves 10

Pine Nut Rice

1 cup pine nuts
butter
2 cups rice, cooked
juice of 1/2 lemon

1/2 cup chopped flat-leaf parsley
salt and pepper to taste
1/2 cup (2 ounces) grated
    Parmesan cheese

Toast the pine nuts in a small amount of butter in a skillet over medium heat until light brown. Combine the pine nuts with the rice in a bowl. Add the lemon juice, parsley, salt and pepper and mix well. Top with the cheese.

Serves 4

Roasted Pepper Rice

3 medium poblano chiles
2 cups chicken broth
2 tablespoons olive oil
1 1/2 cups uncooked white rice
1 small white onion, chopped
2 garlic cloves, minced

salt to taste
3 cups loosely packed sliced
    spinach leaves
1 1/2 cups (6 ounces) crumbled queso
    fresco, goat cheese or feta cheese

Place the poblano chiles on a baking sheet and broil 4 inches from the heat source for 10 minutes or until evenly charred, turning frequently and taking care to char only the skin. Seal in a plastic bag and let stand for 5 minutes. Slip off the blackened skin and chop the poblano chiles into 1/4-inch pieces, discarding the stems and seeds.

Warm the chicken broth in a small saucepan. Heat the olive oil in a medium saucepan with a tight-fitting lid. Add the rice and onion to the olive oil and sauté for 5 minutes or until the rice becomes opaque; do not brown the rice. Add the garlic and sauté for several minutes.

Stir in the warmed broth and roasted poblano chiles; season with salt. Cook, tightly covered, over low heat for 20 minutes. Remove from the heat and sprinkle the spinach over the rice. Replace the lid and let stand for 5 minutes. Test a grain of rice for doneness; add 2 tablespoons water and cook for 5 minutes longer if necessary for the desired doneness. Sprinkle with the cheese and serve immediately.

Serves 6 to 8

Wild Mushroom Risotto

2 tablespoons butter
8 ounces wild mushrooms, sliced,
    about 2½ cups
1 medium yellow onion, finely chopped

1 cup uncooked arborio rice
2 cups chicken broth
¾ cup (3 ounces) grated
    Parmesan cheese

Melt the butter in a 10-inch skillet over medium-high heat. Add the mushrooms and onion and sauté until the onion is tender. Add the rice and stir to coat well.

Add the chicken broth and bring to a boil; stir once. Reduce the heat and simmer, covered, for 20 minutes or until the rice is tender and the liquid is absorbed. Stir in the cheese. Remove from the heat and let stand, covered, for 5 minutes. Fluff with a fork.

Serves 4

Curried Couscous

2 tablespoons unsalted butter
1½ cups water
1½ cup uncooked couscous
¼ cup plain yogurt
¼ cup olive oil
2 teaspoons white wine vinegar
1 teaspoon curry powder
¼ teaspoon turmeric
1½ teaspoons kosher salt

1 teaspoon freshly ground pepper
½ cup grated or finely chopped carrot
½ cup minced flat-leaf parsley
½ cup dried currants, golden raisins or
    dried cranberries
¼ cup blanched sliced almonds
4 scallions with tops, thinly sliced
¼ cup finely chopped red onion

Combine the butter with the water in a saucepan and bring to a boil. Pour over the couscous in a bowl and mix well. Cover tightly and let stand for 5 minutes; fluff with a fork.

Whisk the yogurt, olive oil, vinegar, curry powder, turmeric, kosher salt and pepper in a bowl. Add to the couscous and stir with a fork. Stir in the carrot, parsley, currants, almonds, scallions and onion. Adjust the seasonings and serve at room temperature with chicken and lamb.

You may vary the vegetables to suit your taste.

Serves 6

White Cheese Macaroni

2 tablespoons butter
8 slices bread, crusts trimmed, torn into small pieces
5½ cups milk
6 tablespoons (¾ stick) butter
½ cup flour
3 cups (12 ounces) shredded sharp white Cheddar cheese
1 cup (4 ounces) grated pecorino Romano cheese

¼ teaspoon freshly grated nutmeg
2 teaspoons salt
¼ teaspoon white pepper
¼ teaspoon cayenne pepper
16 ounces uncooked elbow macaroni
1 cup (4 ounces) shredded sharp white Cheddar cheese
¼ cup (1 ounce) grated pecorino Romano cheese

Melt 2 tablespoons butter in a saucepan. Toss with the bread pieces in a bowl. Heat the milk in a saucepan over medium-high heat.

Melt 6 tablespoons butter in a large deep saucepan and heat until bubbly. Stir in the flour and cook for 1 minute, stirring constantly. Whisk in the milk and cook until thickened and smooth, whisking constantly. Remove from the heat. Add 3 cups Cheddar cheese, 1 cup pecorino Romano cheese, the nutmeg, salt, white pepper and cayenne pepper; stir until the cheese melts and the sauce is smooth.

Cook the macaroni al dente in boiling water in a large saucepan. Drain and rinse under cold running water; drain again. Add to the cheese sauce and mix gently.

Spoon into a buttered 3-quart baking dish. Sprinkle with 1 cup Cheddar cheese and ¼ cup pecorino Romano cheese. Top with the buttered bread pieces. Bake at 350 degrees for 30 minutes. Cool for 5 minutes before serving.

Serves 12

Thai Noodles

Spicy Thai Sauce

5 garlic cloves, chopped
1/4 cup chopped gingerroot
1/2 cup vegetable oil
1/2 cup sesame paste
1/2 cup creamy peanut butter
1/2 cup soy sauce
1/4 cup dry sherry or dry white wine

1/4 cup rice wine vinegar
1/4 cup honey
2 tablespoons dark sesame oil
1/2 teaspoon hot chili oil
1/8 teaspoon cayenne pepper
1/2 teaspoon freshly ground black pepper

Pasta

salt to taste
vegetable oil
16 ounces uncooked spaghetti
    or linguini

1 red bell pepper, julienned
1 yellow bell pepper, julienned
3 green onions, sliced diagonally into
    1/2-inch pieces

To *prepare the sauce*, combine the garlic and gingerroot in a food processor. Add the oil, sesame paste, peanut butter, soy sauce, wine, vinegar, honey, sesame oil, chili oil, cayenne pepper and black pepper. Process until puréed.

To *prepare the pasta*, bring a large saucepan of water to a boil; add salt to taste and a small amount of oil. Stir in the pasta and cook al dente; drain. Combine the pasta with 3/4 of the sauce, the bell peppers and green onions in a bowl; toss gently to mix well. Serve warm or at room temperature with the remaining sauce. Serve with grilled chicken or meat.

You may prepare the sauce in advance and store in the refrigerator for up to 1 week. Do not add more of the sauce to the pasta than is needed for a meal, however, as the pasta does not keep well once the sauce is added.

Serves 6 to 8

Florida Applesauce

2 large Florida navel oranges
1 lemon
8 Granny Smith apples, peeled
    and sliced
8 McIntosh, Winesap or Red Delicious
    apples, peeled and sliced

2/3 cup packed light brown sugar
1/2 cup (1 stick) butter
2 teaspoons cinnamon
1/2 teaspoon allspice

Grate the zest of the oranges and lemon into a bowl and squeeze the juice of the oranges and lemon into the bowl. Add the apples and toss to mix well. Add the brown sugar, butter, cinnamon and allspice; mix well.

Spoon into a baking dish. Bake, covered, at 350 degrees for 1 1/2 hours or until the apples are very tender. Whisk until smooth. Serve warm, chilled or at room temperature with roasted chicken or turkey.

You may also serve chilled as a light dessert or warm over pancakes or waffles.

Serves 20

FLORIDA NAVEL ORANGES

The Florida navel orange is considered one of the best oranges produced in Florida. The name comes from their "belly button" indentation at the blossom end of the fruit. The state of Florida is home to more than 70% of the total U.S. crop of navel oranges produced each year, although most are grown for their juice. The peak season for harvesting the oranges is between November and May, with the best crops in the winter months of January through March. They are seedless and section easily, so they are great for eating out of hand. The warm Florida sunshine will burst forth with every bite!

Fried Dill Pickles

2 pints sliced dill pickles
1 egg, lightly beaten
1 tablespoon flour
$^1/_2$ teaspoon hot sauce
1$^1/_2$ cups flour

1 teaspoon garlic powder
$^1/_4$ teaspoon salt
2$^1/_2$ teaspoons ground red pepper
vegetable oil for frying

Drain the dill pickles, reserving $^2/_3$ cup pickle juice. Press the pickles between paper towels to remove the excess moisture. Combine the reserved pickle juice, egg, 1 tablespoon flour and the hot sauce in a bowl and mix well. Mix 1$^1/_2$ cups flour, the garlic powder, salt and red pepper in a bowl.

Heat 1$^1/_2$ inches of oil in a skillet. Dip the pickle slices in the egg mixture and coat with the flour mixture. Add to the heated oil in batches and fry for 2 to 3 minutes or until golden brown, turning once. Drain on paper towels and serve immediately.

Serves 20

Grandmother's Southern Corn Bread Dressing

2 cups cornmeal
1 teaspoon baking powder
1 teaspoon baking soda
$^1/_2$ teaspoon salt
3 eggs, beaten
buttermilk

1 cup chopped celery
1 cup chopped onion
$^1/_4$ teaspoon poultry seasoning
pepper to taste
chicken broth

Mix the cornmeal, baking powder, baking soda and salt in a bowl. Add the eggs and enough buttermilk to make of cake batter consistency, mixing well. Spoon into a greased large cast-iron skillet or round baking pan. Bake at 350 degrees for 30 to 35 minutes or until golden brown. Cool to room temperature. Reduce the oven temperature to 325 degrees.

Crumble the corn bread into a bowl and add the celery, onion, poultry seasoning and pepper; mix well. Add enough chicken broth to make soupy, mixing well. Spoon into a greased 9×13-inch baking dish. Bake at 325 degrees for 40 minutes or until set and golden brown.

Serves 8

Crème Brûlée

Seagars

1 vanilla bean	16 egg yolks, beaten
4 cups heavy cream	sugar for the topping
1 cup half-and-half	4 strawberries, cut into halves
6 ounces sugar	16 raspberries

Cut the vanilla bean into halves lengthwise. Combine with the heavy cream, half-and-half and 6 ounces sugar in a heavy saucepan. Bring just to a simmer. Stir a small amount into the egg yolks, then stir the egg yolks gradually into the heated cream mixture. Remove the vanilla bean. Place in a larger pan of ice to cool.

Strain the cooled mixture into a pitcher and pour into 4 shallow ramekins. Place in a baking pan with sides 2 inches deep. Add enough hot water to reach halfway up the sides of the ramekins. Cover the ramekins with foil.

Bake at 275 degrees for 25 minutes or until set. Cool on a wire rack and chill in the refrigerator until ready to serve.

Mist the tops of the brûlée with water. Sprinkle with sugar, shaking off the excess. Repeat the process. Broil until caramelized golden brown or caramelize with a propane torch, taking care not to overbrown. Cool until the topping is firm. Garnish each with 2 strawberry halves and 2 raspberries.

Serves 4

CAMP WALTON SCHOOLHOUSE

On a tree-shaded corner of First Street in the heart of Downtown Ft. Walton Beach sits a one-room schoolhouse reminiscent of days gone by. This building, constructed in 1911, was the first school constructed for the children of Camp Walton, later to be named Ft. Walton Beach. When it originally opened, eight grades were taught in one schoolroom. The school grew, but was eventually closed in 1936, when the new brick Ft. Walton Grammar School opened. It became an educational museum when the building was adopted and restored by the Junior League of the Emerald Coast in 1976. During the school year, more than 3,000 schoolchildren from five counties visit and get to take a step back in time while learning the history of the area.

Chocolate Flan

Rutherfords 465

Dark Chocolate Flan

1 cup milk
1/4 cup heavy cream
3 ounces chocolate, shaved
1/4 cup sugar
4 egg yolks, beaten

1/2 teaspoon Kahlúa
pinch of cinnamon
2 drops of vanilla extract
2 drops of almond extract

White Chocolate Flan

1/2 cup milk
1/4 cup heavy cream
2 ounces white chocolate, shaved
2 ounces Bailey's Irish cream

3 egg yolks, beaten
1/4 cup sugar
2 drops of vanilla extract

Chocolate Triangles and Assembly

1 pound chocolate, melted
white chocolate, melted
whipped cream

confectioners' sugar
shaved chocolate
fresh berries

To prepare the dark chocolate flan, combine all the ingredients in a bowl and mix well. Spoon into 4- to 6-ounce ramekins and cover with foil. Place in a baking pan and add enough water to reach halfway up the sides of the ramekins. Bake at 300 degrees for 45 minutes. Cool on a wire rack. Chill until serving time.

To prepare the white chocolate flan, combine the milk, cream, white chocolate, Irish cream, egg yolks, sugar and vanilla in a bowl and mix well. Spoon into 2-ounce ramekins and cover with foil. Place in a baking pan and add enough water to reach halfway up the sides of the ramekins. Bake at 275 degrees for 30 minutes. Cool on a wire rack. Chill until serving time.

To prepare the chocolate triangles, spread the melted chocolate on a parchment-lined baking sheet. Chill until firm. Stripe with the white chocolate. Chill until firm. Cut the chocolate into triangles. Chill until serving time.

To assemble, place the dark chocolate flans on serving plates and top each with a chocolate triangle. Place the white chocolate flans on the triangles and top each with a second chocolate triangle. Garnish with whipped cream, confectioners' sugar, shaved chocolate and fresh berries.

Serves 4

Bread Pudding

Pudding

3 eggs
1 1/2 cups sugar
2 tablespoons light brown sugar
1/2 teaspoon nutmeg

1/4 cup (1/2 stick) butter, melted
2 3/4 cups evaporated skim milk
4 cups cubed day-old French bread

Vanilla Sauce

1 cup sugar
2 tablespoons flour
2 cups boiling water

1/4 cup (1/2 stick) butter
2 teaspoons vanilla extract

To prepare the pudding, combine the eggs, sugar, brown sugar and nutmeg in a bowl; beat until smooth. Add the butter and evaporated milk and mix well. Stir in the bread cubes gently.

Spoon into a lightly greased 2-quart baking dish. Bake at 375 degrees for 30 minutes. Cover with foil and bake for 20 to 25 minutes longer or until set. Let stand for 10 minutes before serving.

To prepare the sauce, mix the sugar and flour in a saucepan. Add the boiling water and mix well. Bring to a boil over medium-high heat and boil for 1 minute, stirring constantly. Stir in the butter and vanilla. Serve hot over the bread pudding.

You may prefer to serve the pudding with one of the sauces below.

For Brandy Sauce, dissolve 2 tablespoons cornstarch in 1/4 cup water in a small bowl. Combine 1 cup sugar, 1 cup brandy, 1/2 cup water and 2 tablespoons butter in a small saucepan. Bring to a boil over medium heat. Stir in the cornstarch mixture and cook until thickened, stirring constantly. Serve hot.

For Rum Sauce, combine 1/2 cup (1 stick) butter, 3/4 cup sugar and 1/2 cup half-and-half in a saucepan. Cook for 10 to 15 minutes or until slightly thickened, stirring constantly. Stir in 3 tablespoons rum or 2 teaspoons rum extract, 1 teaspoon vanilla and nutmeg to taste. Serve hot.

Serves 6 to 8

Peaches and Cream

1½ cups flour
2 (4-ounce) packages vanilla instant
   pudding mix
2 teaspoons baking powder
½ teaspoon salt
6 tablespoons (¾ stick) butter,
   partially melted

1 cup milk
1 egg
2 (15-ounce) cans sliced peaches
16 ounces cream cheese, softened
1 cup sugar
2 teaspoons cinnamon
2 tablespoons sugar

Mix the flour, pudding mix, baking powder and salt in a mixing bowl. Add the butter, milk and egg; beat for 2 minutes. Spoon into a 9×13-inch baking dish. Drain the peaches, reserving the juice. Arrange the peaches over the batter in the baking dish.

Combine the reserved peach juice with the cream cheese and 1 cup sugar in a mixing bowl; beat for 2 minutes. Spread over the peaches, covering evenly.

Mix the cinnamon and 2 tablespoons sugar in a bowl. Sprinkle over the top. Bake at 350 degrees for 30 to 35 minutes or until golden brown.

Serves 8 to 10

GARNIER POST OFFICE

Garnier Post Office was the original post office in the area and was located on the beach in Farmer's Bayou in Camp Walton, Florida, which later became Ft. Walton Beach. The original postmaster was Euphrates A. Mooney, who was appointed in 1906. The mail came by boat from Pensacola, overland six miles from Mary Esther, then on to Boggy Bayou by boat. Mrs. Mooney took over the duties after the death of her husband. The Garnier Post Office was eventually abandoned when mail began to be delivered to homes, and it was ultimately doomed for destruction. The Junior League of the Emerald Coast and the City of Ft. Walton Beach restored the post office between 1981 and 1988. It is now part of the museum division and is included in the tour with Camp Walton Schoolhouse.

Tart Shell

7/8 cup (1 3/4 sticks) unsalted butter
2 1/2 cups flour
3 tablespoons sugar

1/8 teaspoon salt
2 egg yolks
5 tablespoons ice water

Combine the butter and flour in a food processor or blender and process until crumbly. Add the sugar and salt and process just until combined. Add the egg yolks and ice water gradually, processing for 20 seconds. Shape the mixture into a ball on a floured surface. Knead the mixture lightly with the heel of your hand, working quickly to keep the dough chilled; do not overknead. Press into a 10-inch tart pan with a removable bottom. Chill for 20 minutes or longer. Line the shell with foil and fill with pie weights or dried beans.

Bake at 350 degrees for 15 minutes. Remove the foil and weights and bake for 5 to 6 minutes longer or until golden brown. Cool on a wire rack. Fill as desired.

You may also bake in two 7 1/2-inch tart pans or a dozen small tart pans. Adjust the baking time accordingly.

Makes 1 (10-inch) tart shell

Rum Apricot Tart

2 eggs
2/3 cup sugar
1/2 cup flour
2 1/2 cups heavy cream
1/2 cup golden rum
4 teaspoons nutmeg

16 to 20 fresh apricots, cut into wedges
2 (10-inch) Tart Shells, partially baked
and cooled (above)
1/4 cup sugar
2 tablespoon unsalted butter, chopped
confectioners' sugar

Combine the eggs and 2/3 cup sugar in a mixing bowl and beat until thick and pale yellow. Add the flour and beat until smooth. Stir in the cream, rum and nutmeg.

Arrange the apricot wedges cut side down in the partially baked Tart Shells. Sprinkle with 1/4 cup sugar and dot with the butter. Bake at 375 degrees for 5 minutes.

Pour the cream mixture evenly over the apricots. Bake for 30 minutes longer or until the filling is set and golden brown. Cool slightly and dust with confectioners' sugar. Broil for several seconds or just until golden brown. Serve warm.

Makes 2 (10-inch) tarts

Lemon Curd Tart

6 egg yolks, beaten
1 cup sugar
¹/₂ cup lemon juice
¹/₂ cup (1 stick) unsalted butter, chopped

1¹/₂ tablespoons grated lemon zest
1 (7¹/₂-inch) Tart Shell, baked and
  cooled (page 188)

Strain the egg yolks through a sieve into a medium saucepan. Add the sugar and lemon juice and mix well. Cook over low heat for 12 minutes or until thickened, stirring constantly. Remove from the heat and stir until the mixture cools slightly. Add the butter 1 piece at a time, mixing until smooth after each addition. Stir in the lemon zest. Cool the mixture completely. Spoon into the Tart Shell and chill until set.

Makes 1 (7¹/₂-inch) tart

Navel Orange Tart

1 cup orange juice
¹/₂ cup lemon juice
1¹/₂ cups sugar
8 to 10 small navel oranges
2 eggs
2 egg yolks
1 cup sugar

¹/₂ cup (1 stick) unsalted butter, slightly
  warmer than room temperature
1 cup ground pecans
¹/₂ cup orange liqueur, such as Cointreau
  or Grand Marnier
1 (10-inch) Tart Shell, baked and cooled
  (page 188)

Mix the orange juice, lemon juice and 1¹/₂ cups sugar in a nonreactive saucepan. Bring to a boil and reduce the heat. Simmer for 15 minutes. Peel the oranges and separate the sections, discarding the membranes and seeds. Add to the juice mixture and simmer until the slices are almost translucent. Remove the slices from the liquid carefully, taking care to leave intact; place on a wire rack to drain. Boil the syrup until reduced to a syrupy consistency.

Combine the eggs, egg yolks and 1 cup sugar in a mixing bowl and beat until thick and pale yellow. Add the butter, pecans and liqueur; mix well. Pour into the Tart Shell. Bake at 375 degrees for 10 minutes or until set. Cool on a wire rack. Brush the tart with a portion of the glaze and arrange the orange slices in a decorative pattern on the top. Brush with the remaining glaze. Chill until serving time.

Makes 1 (10-inch) tart

Strawberry Blitz Torte

Torte Batter

1 cup flour	1/2 cup sugar
1 teaspoon baking powder	4 egg yolks
1/4 teaspoon salt	3 tablespoons milk
1/2 cup (1 stick) butter, softened	1 teaspoon vanilla extract

Meringue

4 egg whites	1 cup sugar
1/2 teaspoon cream of tartar	1/2 teaspoon vanilla extract
1/2 teaspoon salt	

Strawberry Filling

1 cup whipping cream	2 cups sliced fresh strawberries
1/4 cup confectioners' sugar	8 strawberries

To *prepare the torte batter*, sift the flour, baking powder and salt together. Cream the butter and sugar at medium speed in a large mixing bowl until light and fluffy. Beat in the egg yolks. Add the milk and vanilla and mix well. Add the dry ingredients and mix at low speed until smooth. Spoon into 2 greased 8-inch cake pans.

To *prepare the meringue*, combine the egg whites, cream of tartar and salt in a mixing bowl. Beat until soft peaks form. Add the sugar 2 tablespoons at a time, mixing well after each addition and beating until stiff peaks form. Mix in the vanilla. Spread lightly over the batter in the cake pans.

Bake at 350 degrees for 35 minutes or until the torte layers test done and the meringue is golden brown. Cool in the pans for 10 minutes. Loosen from the sides of the pans and remove meringue side up to a wire rack to cool completely.

To *prepare the filling*, whip the cream in a mixing bowl until frothy. Add the confectioners' sugar gradually, beating until soft peaks form. Add the sliced strawberries and mix gently.

Spread the filling over the meringue sides of the torte layers and stack on a serving plate. Top with the whole strawberries. Chill until serving time.

You may wrap the torte well and freeze for up to 2 months.

Serves 12

Tiramisu
Graffiti

4¹/₂ cups brewed espresso,
　at room temperature
1¹/₂ cups sugar
1 cup brandy
24 ounces ladyfingers
6 egg yolks
3 pounds mascarpone cheese, softened

12 ounces semisweet chocolate, shaved
3 cups whipping cream
6 tablespoons confectioners' sugar
1 teaspoon vanilla extract
baking cocoa
shaved chocolate
chocolate sauce

Combine the espresso, sugar and brandy in a mixing bowl and beat until the sugar dissolves. Remove 1 cup of the mixture to a large bowl and reserve. Dip half the ladyfingers 1 at a time in the remaining espresso mixture and arrange over the bottom of a round pan lined with waxed paper.

Add the egg yolks and mascarpone cheese to the reserved 1 cup of espresso mixture. Whisk just until smooth; do not overmix. Spread half the cheese mixture in the prepared pan and top with 6 ounces of the shaved semisweet chocolate. Repeat the process with the remaining ingredients. Cover with waxed paper and chill for 6 hours or longer.

Combine the whipping cream with the confectioners' sugar and vanilla in a mixing bowl. Beat until soft peaks form. Invert the tiramisu onto a serving plate. Spread the whipped cream over the top and side. Dust with baking cocoa and garnish with additional shaved chocolate and a drizzle of chocolate sauce.

To avoid the possibility of salmonella from uncooked egg yolks, you can use an equivalent amount of egg yolk substitute.

Serves 8 to 10

The photograph for this recipe appears on page 182.

Almond Madeleines
Big City Café

8 ounces almond paste
1 cup sugar
3/4 cup (1 1/2 sticks) butter, softened

6 eggs
1 1/4 cups flour
1 teaspoon baking powder

Cream the almond paste and sugar in a mixing bowl until smooth. Add the butter and beat until light. Beat in the eggs 1 at a time. Add the flour and baking powder and mix well. Chill for 2 to 12 hours.

Spoon into lightly greased and lightly floured madeleine molds or small muffin cups, filling half full. Bake at 350 degrees for 15 minutes or until golden brown. Tip the molds immediately to remove the madeleines. Invert decorative side up on a wire rack to cool.

You can also double the recipe and bake in a bundt pan or other cake pan. Fold fresh blackberries or raspberries into the batter and serve warm with berry sauce and whipped cream. Both the batter and baked product can be frozen for fresh warm madeleines any time.

Makes 2 dozen

Double Chip Tassies

3 ounces cream cheese, softened
3/4 cup (1 1/2 sticks) butter, softened
1 1/2 cups flour
1/4 cup sugar
1 egg, lightly beaten
1/2 cup sugar

2 tablespoons butter or margarine, melted
1/4 teaspoon lemon juice
1/4 teaspoon vanilla extract
1 3/4 cups (11 ounces) mixed peanut butter chips and milk chocolate chips
2 teaspoons shortening

Beat the cream cheese and butter in a mixing bowl until light. Add the flour and 1/4 cup sugar and beat until smooth. Chill, covered, for 1 hour or until the dough is firm. Shape the dough into 1-inch balls and press over the bottoms and sides of miniature muffin cups. Mix the next 5 ingredients in a bowl. Reserve 1/3 cup of the peanut butter and milk chocolate chips. Add the remaining chips to the egg mixture. Spoon into the prepared shells.

Bake at 350 degrees for 20 to 25 minutes or until light brown. Cool in the pans and remove to a wire rack. Combine the reserved chips with the shortening in a microwave-safe bowl. Microwave for 30 seconds and stir to blend well. Drizzle over the tassies.

Makes 3 dozen

Key Lime Cheesecake

1¼ cups graham cracker crumbs
2 tablespoons sugar
¼ cup (½ stick) butter or
    margarine, melted
1 teaspoon grated Key lime zest
24 ounces cream cheese, softened
¾ cup sugar
3 eggs

1 tablespoon grated Key lime zest
¼ cup Key lime juice
1 teaspoon vanilla extract
2 cups (16 ounces) sour cream
3 tablespoons sugar
fresh strawberries (optional)
Key lime slices (optional)

Mix the graham cracker crumbs, 2 tablespoons sugar, the butter and 1 teaspoon lime zest in a bowl. Press the mixture evenly over the bottom and up the side of a 9-inch springform pan. Bake at 350 degrees for 5 to 6 minutes or until light brown. Cool on a wire rack.

Beat the cream cheese in a mixing bowl until light. Add ¾ cup sugar gradually, beating until fluffy. Beat in the eggs 1 at a time. Stir in 1 tablespoon lime zest, the lime juice and vanilla. Spoon into the prepared springform pan. Bake at 375 degrees for 45 minutes or until set. Increase the oven temperature to 500 degrees.

Combine the sour cream and 3 tablespoons sugar in a bowl and mix well. Spread evenly over the cheesecake. Bake at 500 degrees for 5 minutes. Cool to room temperature on a wire rack. Chill the cheesecake for 8 hours or longer. Place on a serving plate and remove the side of the springform pan carefully. Top with strawberries and lime slices.

Serves 16

KEY LIMES

Key limes are small tart limes that are grown only in the Florida Keys and Mexico. They have a unique and bitter tartness that gives them a special taste. When Key limes are green, that is the early ripening stage when the flavor is the strongest. The yellow color appears late in the ripening stage when the flavor becomes more mellow. Another unique fact about Key limes is that the trees have big thorns, unlike regular lime trees. The most famous dish made with Key limes is Key lime pie. People have tried to reproduce this with regular limes, and the taste and texture are disappointing. Bottled authentic Key lime juice, used for pies and flavoring, has a shelf life of about four to six months.

Rich and Creamy Cheesecake

1 tablespoon unsalted butter, melted
3 tablespoons graham cracker crumbs
32 ounces cream cheese, softened
1 1/4 cups sugar
4 eggs, at room temperature

1 teaspoon minced lemon zest
2 teaspoons vanilla extract
1/4 cup heavy cream
1/4 cup (2 ounces) sour cream

Line the detached bottom of a 9-inch springform pan with foil. Tuck the foil under the pan bottom and attach the side of the pan; press the foil back up around the side of the pan. Brush the bottom and side of the pan with the butter and sprinkle with the graham cracker crumbs, tilting the pan to coat evenly. Line the outside of the pan with heavy-duty foil and place in a larger baking pan.

Beat the cream cheese in a mixing bowl until light. Add the sugar gradually, beating at medium speed for 3 minutes or until fluffy. Beat in the eggs 1 at a time, scraping down the side of the bowl after each addition. Add the lemon zest and vanilla and mix well. Stir in the cream and sour cream.

Spoon into the springform pan. Place the baking pan on the center oven rack and add enough boiling water to reach halfway up the side of the springform pan. Bake at 325 degrees for 55 to 60 minutes or until the edge of the cheesecake is set but the center still jiggles when the pan is tapped.

Turn off the oven and let the cheesecake stand in the oven with the door ajar for 1 hour. Remove to a wire rack to cool completely. Chill, covered, in the refrigerator for up to 4 days. Place on a serving plate and remove the side of the pan.

Serves 16

The photograph for this recipe appears on page 182.

Toffee Crunch Cheesecake

Cheesecake Crust

1¹/₂ cups graham cracker crumbs
6 tablespoons (³/₄ stick) butter, melted

2 tablespoons brown sugar
¹/₂ teaspoon vanilla extract

Filling

24 ounces cream cheese, softened
1 cup sugar
2 tablespoons vanilla extract
1 cup (8 ounces) sour cream

3 eggs
1¹/₄ cups coarsely crushed chocolate-
    covered toffee candy bars

Toffee Topping

1¹/₂ cups (12 ounces) sour cream
¹/₄ cup sugar
2 teaspoons vanilla extract

coarsely chopped chocolate-covered
    toffee candy bars

To *prepare the crust*, mix the graham cracker crumbs, butter, brown sugar and vanilla in a food processor and process until mixed. Press over the bottom and 2 inches up the side of a buttered 9-inch springform pan.

To *prepare the filling*, combine the cream cheese, sugar and vanilla in a large mixing bowl and beat until light and fluffy. Beat in the sour cream. Beat in the eggs 1 at a time. Sprinkle the crushed candy in the prepared springform pan. Spoon the cream cheese mixture evenly over the candy.

Bake at 350 degrees for 1 hour and 5 minutes or until the filling is cracked around the edge and just set in the center. Cool on a wire rack for 10 minutes; the center of the filling will fall.

To *prepare the topping*, combine the sour cream, sugar and vanilla in a medium bowl and mix well. Spread over the cheesecake. Bake for 5 minutes longer or just until the topping sets. Chill for 8 hours or longer.

Loosen the cheesecake from the side of the springform pan with a knife. Place on a serving plate and remove the side of the pan. Sprinkle with additional candy.

Serves 16

Delta Mud Cake

Cake

1 cup (2 sticks) butter, melted
1/2 cup baking cocoa
4 eggs, lightly beaten
2 cups sugar
1 1/2 cups flour

1 1/2 cups finely chopped macadamias
   or pecans
1 teaspoon vanilla extract
1/2 teaspoon salt

Topping

marshmallows
1 (1-pound) package
   confectioners' sugar
1/2 cup milk

1/3 cup baking cocoa
1/2 cup (1 stick) butter, softened
chopped macadamias or pecans

To prepare the cake, blend the butter and baking cocoa in a mixing bowl. Beat in the eggs and sugar. Add the flour, macadamias, vanilla and salt; mix well. Spoon into a greased 9×13-inch baking pan. Bake at 350 degrees for 35 minutes.

   To prepare the topping, sprinkle enough marshmallows over the cake to cover completely. Place in a 350-degree oven just until the marshmallows melt. Combine the confectioners' sugar, milk, baking cocoa and butter in a mixing bowl; mix until smooth. Spread over the marshmallows. Top with additional macadamias.

Serves 16

Four-Fudge Bundt Cake

Cake

1 cup (2 sticks) butter, softened
1 1/2 cups sugar
4 eggs
1/2 teaspoon baking soda
1 cup buttermilk
2 1/2 cups flour

1 cup (6 ounces) semisweet
   chocolate chips
2 (4-ounce) bars milk chocolate, melted
   and cooled
1/3 cup chocolate syrup
2 teaspoons vanilla extract

Two-Chocolate Glaze

4 ounces white chocolate, chopped
2 tablespoons plus
   2 teaspoons shortening

1/2 cup (3 ounces) semisweet
   chocolate chips

To *prepare the cake*, cream the butter in a mixing bowl until light. Add the sugar gradually, beating at medium speed until fluffy. Beat in the eggs 1 at a time. Dissolve the baking soda in the buttermilk. Add to the creamed mixture alternately with the flour, mixing well after each addition. Stir in the remaining ingredients. Spoon into a 10-inch bundt pan that has been generously greased and dusted with baking cocoa. Bake at 300 degrees for 1 hour and 20 to 25 minutes or until the cake tests done. Invert onto a serving plate to cool.

   To *prepare the glaze*, combine the white chocolate and 2 tablespoons of the shortening in a double boiler. Heat until melted, stirring to blend well. Drizzle over the cooled cake. Melt the chocolate chips with the remaining shortening in a double boiler, stirring until smooth. Drizzle over the white chocolate.

Serves 16

The photograph for this recipe appears on page 182.

Italian Cream Cake
Texas Governor's Mansion

Cake

5 extra-large egg whites,
   at room temperature
½ cup sugar
½ cup (1 stick) butter, softened
½ cup (1 stick) margarine, softened
1½ cups sugar
½ teaspoon salt
1½ teaspoons vanilla extract

5 extra-large egg yolks,
   at room temperature
1 teaspoon baking soda
1 cup buttermilk, at room temperature
2 cups flour
1 cup finely chopped pecans
1 (3-ounce) can flaked coconut

Italian Cream Frosting

¾ cup (1½ sticks) butter, softened
12 ounces cream cheese, softened
1½ teaspoons vanilla extract

1½ (1-pound) packages
   confectioners' sugar

To prepare the cake, beat the egg whites in a mixing bowl until soft peaks form. Add ½ cup sugar gradually, beating constantly until stiff peaks form.

Cream the butter, margarine, 1½ cups sugar, the salt and vanilla in a mixing bowl until light and fluffy. Beat in the egg yolks 1 at a time. Dissolve the baking soda in the buttermilk. Add to the creamed mixture alternately with the flour, beginning and ending with the flour and mixing well after each addition. Fold in the beaten egg whites, pecans and coconut.

Spoon the batter into three 9-inch cake pans with greased and floured bottoms. Bake at 325 degrees for 40 minutes. Cool in the pans for 10 minutes and remove to a wire rack to cool completely.

To prepare the frosting, combine the butter, cream cheese and vanilla in a mixing bowl and beat until light. Add the confectioners' sugar and beat until fluffy. Spread between the layers and over the top and side of the cake. Store in the refrigerator.

Serves 16 to 20

Kahlúa Cake

Cake

3 ounces white chocolate, chopped	1/2 cup (1 stick) butter, softened
3 tablespoons Kahlúa	2 tablespoons shortening
2 tablespoons vodka	1 1/4 cups sugar
2 cups sifted cake flour	3 eggs
1/2 teaspoon baking powder	3/4 cup buttermilk
3/4 teaspoon baking soda	1/3 cup apricot jam

Kahlúa Cream

2 cups whipping cream	2 teaspoons vodka
1/3 cup sifted confectioners' sugar	white chocolate shavings or curls
1/3 cup Kahlúa	

To *prepare the cake*, combine the white chocolate with the Kahlúa and vodka in a double boiler. Heat until the chocolate melts, stirring to blend well. Cool slightly.

Sift the flour, baking powder and baking soda together. Cream the butter, shortening and sugar in a large mixing bowl until light and fluffy. Beat in the eggs 1 at a time. Fold in the white chocolate mixture. Add the dry ingredients alternately with the buttermilk, mixing well after each addition.

Spoon into 2 greased and floured 9-inch cake pans. Bake at 350 degrees for 25 to 30 minutes or until a tester inserted into the center comes out clean. Cool in the pans for 10 minutes. Remove to a wire rack to cool completely. Brush each cooled layer with half the apricot jam.

To *prepare the cream*, beat the whipping cream with the confectioners' sugar in a mixing bowl until thickened. Add the Kahlúa and vodka gradually, beating constantly until soft peaks form.

Spread 1 cake layer with 1/4 cup of the cream and top with the second cake layer. Spread the remaining cream over the top and side of the cake. Garnish with white chocolate. Store in the refrigerator, allowing to stand at room temperature for 30 minutes before serving.

Serves 12 to 16

Glazed Lemon Pound Cake

Cake

3 cups flour
½ teaspoon baking powder
½ teaspoon salt
1 cup (2 sticks) margarine, softened
½ cup shortening
3 cups sugar

5 eggs, beaten
1 cup milk
1 teaspoon vanilla extract
1 teaspoon lemon extract
2½ teaspoons grated lemon zest

Lemon Glaze

6 tablespoons (¾ stick) butter, softened
1 cup sugar

3 tablespoons lemon juice
3 tablespoons water

To *prepare the cake*, mix the flour, baking powder and salt together. Cream the margarine and shortening in a mixing bowl until light. Add the sugar and beat until fluffy. Beat in the eggs. Add the dry ingredients alternately with the milk, mixing well after each addition. Stir in the flavorings and lemon zest.

Spoon into a greased and floured tube pan. Bake at 325 degrees for 1½ hours or until the cake tests done.

To *prepare the glaze*, melt the butter in a small saucepan. Add the sugar, lemon juice and water. Cook for 5 minutes or until the sugar dissolves, stirring to mix well.

Pierce holes in the cake while still in the pan. Pour the glaze over the cake and cool on a wire rack. Remove to a serving plate.

Serves 16

Coconut Cream Cheese Pound Cake

3 cups flour
1/4 teaspoon baking soda
1/4 teaspoon salt
1/2 cup (1 stick) butter, softened
1/2 cup shortening
8 ounces cream cheese, softened

3 cups sugar
6 eggs
1 (16-ounce) package frozen
  coconut, thawed
1 teaspoon vanilla extract
1 teaspoon coconut extract

Mix the flour, baking soda and salt together. Cream the butter, shortening and cream cheese in a mixing bowl until light. Add the sugar gradually, beating at medium speed until fluffy. Beat in the eggs 1 at a time. Add the dry ingredients and mix just until blended. Stir in the coconut and flavorings.

Spoon into a greased and floured 10-inch tube pan. Bake at 350 degrees for 1 1/4 hours. Cool in the pan for 10 minutes. Invert onto a wire rack to cool completely.

Serves 16

Easy Chocolate Frosting

2 tablespoons butter
1/2 cup (3 ounces) semisweet
  chocolate chips

1/3 cup milk
2 cups sifted confectioners' sugar

Melt the butter in a saucepan. Add the chocolate chips and milk and cook over low heat until the chips melt, stirring constantly to blend well. Add the confectioners' sugar gradually, beating constantly until smooth.

Makes 1 cup

Praline Carrot Cake

Cake

3 cups grated carrots
2 cups flour
1 teaspoon baking powder
2 teaspoons baking soda
2 cups sugar

1 teaspoon cinnamon
$1/2$ teaspoon salt
4 eggs, beaten
$1^{1}/_{4}$ cups vegetable oil
1 cup chopped pecans

Cream Cheese Frosting

$1/2$ cup (1 stick) butter, softened
8 ounces cream cheese, softened
1 (1-pound) package
   confectioners' sugar

1 teaspoon cinnamon
1 teaspoon vanilla extract

Assembly

Praline Sauce (page 203)   **Candied Pecans (page 203)**

To *prepare the cake*, combine the carrots, flour, baking powder, baking soda, sugar, cinnamon and salt in a large bowl; mix well. Stir in the eggs, oil and pecans.

Spoon into 3 greased and floured 9-inch cake pans. Bake at 350 degrees for 30 minutes or until a wooden pick inserted in the center comes out clean. Cool in the pans for 10 minutes. Remove to a wire rack to cool completely.

To *prepare the frosting*, cream the butter and cream cheese in a mixing bowl until light. Add the confectioners' sugar, cinnamon and vanilla and beat until fluffy.

To assemble the cake, place 1 of the cooled cake layers rounded side down on a cake plate. Pipe or spoon 1 cup of the frosting in a rim 1 inch wide and $1/2$ inch high around the outer edge of the layer. Spoon 2 tablespoons of the frosting in the center of the layer and spread, leaving an unfrosted ring between the 2 applications of frosting.

Spoon half the Praline Sauce into the unfrosted area and spread evenly. Add a second cake layer rounded side up. Repeat the steps with the frosting and Praline Sauce. Top with the third cake layer. Spread the remaining frosting over the top and side of the cake. Arrange the Candied Pecans over the top of the cake.

Serves 16

Praline Sauce

6 tablespoons (³/₄ stick) butter
6 tablespoons brown sugar

¹/₄ cup heavy cream
2 teaspoons vanilla extract

Melt the butter in a small saucepan over medium heat. Stir in the brown sugar and cream. Bring to a boil, stirring constantly. Reduce the heat and simmer for 3 minutes, stirring occasionally. Stir in the vanilla. Cool to room temperature.

Makes ²/₃ cup

Candied Pecans

¹/₃ cup packed brown sugar
1 tablespoon orange juice

¹/₂ cup pecan halves

Blend the brown sugar and orange juice in a small bowl. Stir in the pecan halves, coating well. Spread in a lightly greased 8×8-inch baking pan. Bake at 350 degrees for 12 minutes or until the pecans are brown and the syrup is bubbly, stirring once. Spread on a lightly greased tray and separate into individual pecans. Cool to room temperature on a wire rack.

Makes ¹/₂ cup

The photograph for this recipe appears on page 182.

Strawberry Cream Angel Food Cake

Cake

1 cup cake flour

²/₃ cup sugar

13 egg whites, about 1³/₄ cups,
   at room temperature

1 teaspoon cream of tartar

¹/₂ teaspoon salt

1 teaspoon almond extract, or to taste

1 cup sugar

Filling

8 ounces cream cheese, softened

1 (14-ounce) can sweetened
   condensed milk

¹/₃ cup lemon juice

2 teaspoons almond liqueur

2¹/₂ cups sliced fresh strawberries

Whipped Cream Frosting

¹/₂ cup whipping cream

2 teaspoons cornstarch

¹/₄ cup confectioners' sugar

4 teaspoons almond liqueur

1¹/₂ cups whipping cream

To *prepare the cake*, sift the flour 3 times. Add ²/₃ cup sugar and sift again. Beat the egg whites in a large mixing bowl just until mixed. Add the cream of tartar and salt and beat until frothy. Add the almond extract and 1 cup sugar gradually, beating constantly until soft peaks form. Sift the flour mixture over the egg whites ¹/₄ at a time, folding in after each addition. Spoon into an ungreased 10-inch tube pan with a removable bottom. Rap the pan on a hard surface to remove any air bubbles. Bake at 300 degrees on the center oven rack for 1 hour or until the cake springs back when lightly touched. Invert onto the neck of a bottle to cool completely. Remove the cake from the pan; cut a 1-inch slice from the top with a serrated knife. Make a cut along the inner and outer edges of the cake. Hollow out between the 2 cuts. Tear the removed cake into bite-size pieces.

To *prepare the filling*, beat the cream cheese in a mixing bowl until light. Beat in the sweetened condensed milk. Stir in the lemon juice and liqueur. Fold in the cake pieces and strawberries. Spoon into the cake; replace the top. Chill, covered with plastic wrap, for 8 hours or longer.

To *prepare the frosting*, combine ¹/₂ cup whipping cream with the cornstarch and confectioners' sugar in a heavy saucepan. Bring to a boil and cook until thickened, stirring constantly. Cool to room temperature. Stir in the liqueur. Beat 1¹/₂ cups whipping cream in a mixing bowl until tracks from the beater hold. Add the cooled cornstarch mixture and beat until firm peaks form. Spread over the filled cake. Chill until serving time.

Serves 12

Black Bottom Key Lime Pie

1¼ cups chocolate wafer crumbs
¼ cup (½ stick) butter, softened
1 (14-ounce) can sweetened
  condensed milk
½ cup Key lime juice

4 egg yolks
½ teaspoon vanilla extract
1 cup whipping cream
3 tablespoons sugar
grated Key lime zest

Mix the chocolate wafer crumbs with the butter in a bowl. Press over the bottom and side of a 9-inch pie plate. Bake at 375 degrees for 8 minutes. Cool on a wire rack.

Combine the sweetened condensed milk, Key lime juice, egg yolks and vanilla in a mixing bowl and mix until smooth. Spoon into the cooled crust and bake for 8 minutes. Cool on a wire rack.

Beat the whipping cream in a mixing bowl until frothy. Add the sugar gradually, beating constantly until soft peaks form. Spoon over the top of the pie. Chill until serving time. Garnish with lime zest.

Serves 6 to 8

The photograph for this recipe appears on page 182.

Chocolate Chess Pie

½ cup sugar
1 cup packed brown sugar
1 teaspoon flour
⅛ teaspoon salt
2 eggs
2 tablespoons milk

1 teaspoon vanilla extract
½ cup (1 stick) butter
4 (1-ounce) squares
  unsweetened chocolate
1 cup chopped pecans
1 unbaked (9-inch) deep-dish pie shell

Combine the sugar, brown sugar, flour and salt in a bowl. Add the eggs, milk and vanilla and mix well. Combine the butter with the chocolate in a microwave-safe bowl. Microwave just until melted; stir to blend well. Add to the sugar mixture and mix well. Stir in the pecans.

Spoon into the pie shell. Bake at 350 degrees for 40 minutes. Cool for 15 minutes before serving. Serve with ice cream or whipped cream.

Serves 6 to 8

Crunchy Caramel Apple Pie

Crumb Topping

1 cup packed brown sugar

$^1/_2$ cup flour

$^1/_2$ cup quick-cooking oats

$^1/_2$ cup (1 stick) butter

Pie

$^1/_2$ cup sugar

3 tablespoons flour

1 teaspoon cinnamon

$^1/_8$ teaspoon salt

6 cups thinly sliced Fuji apples or
   Granny Smith apples

1 unbaked (9-inch) pie shell

$^1/_2$ cup chopped pecans

$^1/_4$ cup caramel sauce

To *prepare the crumb topping*, mix the brown sugar, flour and oats in a bowl. Cut in the butter until the mixture resembles coarse crumbs.

To *prepare the pie*, mix the sugar, flour, cinnamon and salt in a bowl. Add the apple slices and toss gently to coat well. Spread the apples in the pie shell. Sprinkle with the crumb topping. Place on a baking sheet and cover the edge with foil.

Bake at 375 degrees for 25 minutes. Remove the foil and bake for 25 to 30 minutes longer or until golden brown. Sprinkle with the pecans and drizzle with the caramel sauce. Serve warm or at room temperature.

Serves 6 to 8

Mocha Fudge Pie

Mocha Fudge Crust

2 teaspoons instant coffee granules
¹/₃ cup hot water
2 cups light fudge brownie mix

1 teaspoon vanilla extract
2 egg whites

Filling

³/₄ cup milk
2 tablespoons coffee liqueur
1 teaspoon instant coffee granules
1 teaspoon vanilla extract

1 (4-ounce) package chocolate instant
  pudding mix
1 ¹/₂ cups whipped topping

Mocha Topping

1 teaspoon instant coffee granules
1 tablespoon coffee liqueur

1 ¹/₂ cups whipped topping
chocolate curls

To *prepare the crust*, dissolve the coffee granules in the hot water in a medium bowl. Add the brownie mix, vanilla and egg whites and mix well. Spread in a 9-inch pie plate sprayed with nonstick cooking spray. Bake at 325 degrees for 22 minutes. Cool on a wire rack.

To *prepare the filling*, combine the milk, liqueur, coffee granules, vanilla and pudding mix in a mixing bowl. Beat at medium speed for 1 minute. Fold in the whipped topping. Spread in the crust.

To *prepare the topping*, dissolve the coffee granules in the liqueur in a bowl. Fold in the whipped topping. Spread over the pudding mixture. Garnish with chocolate curls. Serve immediately or chill, loosely covered, until serving time.

Serves 8

Peanut Butter Pie

1 cup creamy peanut butter
8 ounces cream cheese, softened
1 cup sugar
2 tablespoons butter, melted
1 teaspoon vanilla extract
1 cup whipping cream

1 (9-inch) deep-dish graham cracker
   pie shell
1/2 cup (3 ounces) semisweet
   chocolate chips
1 teaspoon shortening
6 ounces chopped unsalted peanuts

Combine the peanut butter, cream cheese, sugar, butter and vanilla in a large mixing bowl and mix until smooth and creamy.

Beat the whipping cream in a mixing bowl until soft peaks form. Add the peanut butter mixture gradually, mixing well until smooth. Spoon into the pie shell. Chill for 8 hours or longer.

Melt the chocolate chips with the shortening in a saucepan, stirring to blend well. Spread evenly over the pie and sprinkle with the peanuts. Chill until the chocolate is firm.

Serves 6 to 8

Pineapple Coconut Chess Pie

1 1/2 cups sugar
3 tablespoons cornmeal
2 tablespoons flour
1/4 teaspoon salt
4 eggs, lightly beaten
1 teaspoon vanilla extract

1/4 cup (1/2 stick) butter, melted
1 (16-ounce) can crushed
   pineapple, drained
1 (3-ounce) can flaked coconut
1 unbaked (9-inch) pie shell

Mix the sugar, cornmeal, flour and salt in a mixing bowl. Add the eggs and vanilla and mix well. Stir in the butter, pineapple and coconut.

Spoon into the pie shell. Bake at 350 degrees for 40 minutes. Cover with foil and bake for 20 minutes longer or until set. Cool on a wire rack.

Serves 6 to 8

Brownies with Chocolate Chip Cheesecake Topping

Brownies

1¼ cups semisweet chocolate chips
¼ cup (½ stick) butter, softened
½ cup sugar
2 eggs

1 teaspoon vanilla extract
½ teaspoon salt
⅔ cup flour

Chocolate Chip Cheesecake Topping

8 ounces cream cheese, softened
2 tablespoons butter, softened
½ cup sugar
2 eggs

2 tablespoons whole or skim milk
1 tablespoon flour
1 tablespoon vanilla extract
¾ cup semisweet chocolate chips

To *prepare the brownies*, melt the chocolate chips in a double boiler over hot water, stirring until smooth. Cream the butter and sugar in a large mixing bowl until light and fluffy. Beat in the eggs, vanilla and salt. Add the melted chocolate and flour; mix well. Spread in a foil-lined 9×9-inch baking pan.

To *prepare the topping*, combine the cream cheese, butter and sugar in a large mixing bowl. Beat until smooth. Add the eggs, milk, flour and vanilla; mix well. Stir in the chocolate chips. Spread over the brownie layer.

Bake the brownies at 350 degrees for 40 to 45 minutes or until they begin to pull away from the sides of the pan. Cool on a wire rack. Chill in the refrigerator for 8 hours or longer; the topping should be firm. Cut into 2¼-inch squares to serve.

Makes 16

THE MULLET FESTIVAL

The Mullet Festival is a much-anticipated event held every October in Niceville. Known for featuring the local fish, the mullet, this festival is a family event that includes pony rides, country music, and lots of fairground-type foods. Mullet is actually an ancient fish that was cultivated on the Nile River and sought after by the Romans.

Pecan Pie Bars

Crust
4 1/2 cups flour
1/2 teaspoon baking powder
1/4 teaspoon salt
2 cups (4 sticks) unsalted butter, softened
3/4 cup sugar
3 eggs
1 teaspoon vanilla extract

Pecan Filling
2 cups (4 sticks) unsalted butter
1 cup honey
3 cups packed light brown sugar
1 1/4 teaspoons grated orange zest
1 1/4 teaspoons grated lemon zest
1/4 cup heavy cream
6 cups pecans

To *prepare the crust*, sift the flour, baking powder and salt together. Cream the butter and sugar in a mixing bowl for 3 minutes or until light and fluffy. Beat in the eggs 1 at a time. Add the vanilla and mix well. Add the dry ingredients and mix at low speed just until combined to form a dough.

Place on an ungreased cookie sheet. Sprinkle dough and hands lightly with flour and press the dough into a large rectangle, shaping a rim around the edges. Bake at 350 degrees for 15 minutes or until firm but not brown. Cool on a wire rack.

To *prepare the filling*, melt the butter in a large saucepan over low heat. Stir in the honey, brown sugar, orange zest and lemon zest. Increase the heat to medium-high and bring to a boil. Boil for 3 minutes. Remove from the heat and stir in the cream and pecans.

Spread the filling over the cooled crust. Bake for 30 minutes or until the filling is set. Cool on a wire rack. Wrap well and chill in the refrigerator. Cut into bars to serve.

Serves 24

Peanut Butter and Jelly Bars

3 cups flour
1 teaspoon baking powder
1 1/2 teaspoons salt
1 cup (2 sticks) unsalted butter, softened
1 1/2 cups sugar

2 eggs
2 1/2 cups creamy peanut butter
1 teaspoon vanilla extract
2 cups strawberry preserves
2/3 cup coarsely chopped salted peanuts

Grease a 9×13-inch baking pan with butter and line the bottom with baking parchment. Grease the parchment and flour the pan. Whisk the flour, baking powder and salt together.

Cream the butter and sugar at medium speed in a mixing bowl fitted with the paddle attachment for 2 minutes or until light and fluffy. Add the eggs and peanut butter and beat at medium speed for 2 minutes. Add the dry ingredients and mix at low speed until combined. Beat in the vanilla.

Spread 2/3 of the mixture in the baking pan with a spatula. Spread with the preserves. Dollop the remaining peanut butter batter over the preserves and sprinkle with the peanuts. Bake at 350 degrees for 45 minutes. Cool on a wire rack. Cut into 1 1/2×2-inch bars.

Makes 3 dozen

Cinnamon Crisps

1 cup (2 sticks) butter, softened
1 cup sugar
1 egg yolk
1 teaspoon vanilla extract
2 cups flour
2 teaspoons cinnamon

1/2 teaspoon nutmeg
1/4 teaspoon almond extract
1/4 teaspoon butter flavoring
1 egg white
1/2 cup sliced almonds

Cream the butter and sugar in a mixing bowl until light and fluffly. Beat in the egg yolk and vanilla. Add the flour, cinnamon, nutmeg, almond extract and butter flavoring; mix to form a stiff dough. Press the dough into an ungreased 10×15-inch cookie sheet. Spread the unbeaten egg white over the top with your fingertips; pour off any excess egg white. Sprinkle with the almonds, pressing them in lightly. Bake at 250 degrees for 1 hour. Cut immediately into 2-inch squares.

Makes 35

Hazelnut Cookies

¾ cup sliced hazelnuts
½ cup (1 stick) unsalted butter, softened
½ cup packed dark brown sugar
1 teaspoon vanilla extract

1 egg
¾ cup flour
confectioners' sugar (optional)

Spread the hazelnuts on a baking sheet. Toast at 350 degrees for 3 to 4 minutes or until light brown. Cool to room temperature. Increase the oven temperature to 375 degrees.

Cream the butter and brown sugar in a mixing bowl until light and fluffy. Beat in the vanilla and egg. Add the flour gradually and beat until smooth. Stir in the hazelnuts.

Drop by teaspoonfuls 1 inch apart onto 2 ungreased cookie sheets. Bake at 350 degrees for 6 to 8 minutes or until golden brown. Remove to a wire rack to cool. Dust with confectioners' sugar if desired.

Makes 3 dozen

Candy Cookies

3 eggs
1 cup sugar
1 cup packed light brown sugar
½ cup (1 stick) unsalted butter, softened
1½ cups chunky or creamy
      peanut butter

2 teaspoons baking soda
2 teaspoons vanilla extract
4½ cups rolled oats
8 ounces semisweet chocolate chips
8 ounces "M & M's" plain or peanut
      chocolate candies

Whisk the eggs in a large bowl. Add the sugar, brown sugar, butter, peanut butter, baking soda and vanilla 1 ingredient at a time, mixing well after each addition. Stir in the oats, chocolate chips and candies.

Shape by large tablespoonfuls or an ice cream scoop into balls. Place 4 inches apart on an ungreased cookie sheet. Bake at 350 degrees for 12 to 15 minutes or just until golden brown; do not overbake. Remove to a wire rack to cool.

Makes 3 dozen

Orange Lace Cookies

1/4 cup light corn syrup
1/4 cup packed light brown sugar
1/4 cup (1/2 stick) unsalted butter
1 tablespoon Cointreau

1/2 cup plus 2 tablespoons cake flour
1 tablespoon finely chopped orange zest
1 teaspoon salt

Combine the corn syrup, brown sugar, butter and Cointreau in a small saucepan. Cook over low heat until the butter melts, stirring to mix well. Remove from the heat and add the flour, orange zest and salt; mix well.

Drop by heaping teaspoonfuls 2 1/2 inches apart on a cookie sheet lined with baking parchment. Bake at 350 degrees for 12 to 14 minutes or until golden brown; cookies will spread out and bubble.

Let stand on the cookie sheet for 4 to 5 minutes. Remove to a wire rack to cool completely. Stir the batter each time before dropping onto the cookie sheet if baking in batches.

Makes 3 dozen

Sugar Beach Cookies

1 cup (2 sticks) butter, softened
2 cups sugar
3 eggs
4 cups flour, sifted

2 teaspoons baking powder
1 teaspoon vanilla extract
1 teaspoon almond extract
sugar

Cream the butter and 2 cups sugar in a mixing bowl until light and fluffy. Beat in the eggs. Add the flour, baking powder and flavorings; mix to form a dough. Chill until firm.

Roll 1/4 of the dough at a time to a thickness of 1/8 inch on a floured surface; leave the unused portion of the dough in the refrigerator. Cut as desired with cookie cutters.

Place the cookies on a cookie sheet. Bake at 325 degrees for 10 minutes or until light brown. Sprinkle with colored or Sugar Beach white sugar. Cool on a wire rack.

Makes 4 dozen

Double Chocolate Hazelnut Biscotti

½ cup hazelnuts
1¾ cups flour
½ cup (3 ounces) miniature semisweet
  chocolate chips
½ cup baking cocoa
1 tablespoon instant coffee granules

1 teaspoon baking soda
½ teaspoon salt
1 cup sugar
2 eggs
2 egg whites
2 teaspoons vanilla extract

Spread the hazelnuts on a baking sheet. Toast at 350 degrees for 8 minutes, watching carefully to prevent burning. Cool to room temperature. Line 2 cookie sheets with foil and spray the foil with nonstick cooking spray.

Combine 2 tablespoons of the hazelnuts with the flour, 2 tablespoons of the chocolate chips, the baking cocoa, coffee granules, baking soda and salt in a food processor. Process until finely ground. Remove to a bowl.

Add the sugar, eggs, egg whites and vanilla to the food processor. Process until slightly thickened. Add the flour mixture and process until smooth. Combine with the remaining hazelnuts and chocolate chips in a bowl and mix with a spoon.

Shape into 4 logs 1½ inches wide and 14 inches long. Place on the prepared cookie sheets. Bake at 350 degrees for 15 minutes. Remove from the oven and reduce the oven temperature to 300 degrees.

Slice the logs diagonally into ½-inch slices with a serrated knife. Stand the slices upright 1 inch apart on a cookie sheet. Bake at 300 degrees for 20 to 25 minutes or until golden brown. Remove to a wire rack to cool.

Serves 20

Buckeyes

1¼ cups (2½ sticks) butter, softened
1 (18-ounce) jar creamy peanut butter
7 cups sifted confectioners' sugar

3 cups (18 ounces) semisweet
    chocolate chips
1½ tablespoons shortening

Process the butter and peanut butter in a food processor until blended. Add 3 cups of the confectioners' sugar and process until smooth. Add the remaining confectioners' sugar gradually, processing until the mixture pulls away from the side of the container after each addition. Process until no longer crumbly. Shape into 1-inch balls. Chill, covered, in the refrigerator.

Combine the chocolate chips and shortening in a double boiler. Heat over simmering water until the chocolate and shortening melt, stirring to blend well. Remove the double boiler from the heat, leaving the top of the boiler over the hot water.

Dip each candy ball into the chocolate mixture with a wooden pick, coating ¾ of the ball. Place on waxed paper to cool, smoothing over the hole left by the pick. Let stand until the chocolate is firm. Store in an airtight container in the refrigerator.

Makes 8 dozen

Pralines

2 cups sugar
1 cup milk
1 tablespoon butter

¼ teaspoon baking soda
½ teaspoon salt
1 cup chopped pecans

Combine the sugar, milk, butter, baking soda and salt in a heavy cast-iron skillet. Bring to a boil, stirring to blend well. Stir in the pecans and boil over low to medium heat for 15 minutes. Remove from the heat and beat with a wooden spoon or heavy-duty hand mixer on low speed until the mixture becomes a light creamy color. Drop by 3 tablespoonfuls onto waxed paper. Let stand until firm.

Makes 12

Contributors

Shannon Aden
Jennifer Amiel
Michelle Anchors
Angler's Beachside Café
Jane Ballard
Callie Barker
Patricia Barnes
Nan Barrow
Jane Barton
Beachwalk Café
Julie Beaty
Chef Andi Bell
Jean Courtney Belue
Claire Benz
Big City Café
Blues
Anna Lee Bonds
Lacy Bonjean
Jean Bowman
Marilyn Brannon
Holly Brelia
Charlene Bremer
Rich Bremer
Elizabeth Ward
    Browning
Kim Brundage

Lisa Buchman
Laurie Carbonara
Dee Dee Carr
Linda Carr
Anne Caulfield
Liz Cavanah
Carrie Chavers
Katherine Chase
Cathy Clarke
Ann Coleman
Paige Collier
Erin Copley
Charla Cotton
Julie Dubuisson Cotton
Keary Couget
Alice Davis
Nancy Davis
Becky Destin
Dewey Destin Seafood
    Restaurant
Gary Dubuisson
Chef Bill Durand
Jennifer Esses
Gonzolo Fernandez
Jamie Fields
Mary Finlay

Iris Finn
Flamingo Café
Cindy Frakes
Diane Fraser
Pat Fulwiler
Catherine Garvie
Niki Garvie
Jeri Ghosh
Susan Gillen
Rita Goldman
Gourmet Entrees to Go
Graffiti's
Jennifer Griffin
Mary Grimsley
Guiseppi's Wharf
Erin Hansen
Harry T's Boathouse
Pamela Herman
Julie Howell
Cici Hruby
Kerry Huffman
Becky Hunt
Steve Hunt
Jamie Jones
Nancy Jordan
Anna Bonds Kessler

Mary Starnes King

Chef Jason Knoll

Judy Lee

Henrietta Maltezo

Caroline Maney

Jamie Martin

Bettie Rae Mattern

Chef Bruce McAdoo

Louis McAdoo

Nikki Mean

Judy Morris

Karen Morris

Donna Munch

Susan Murphree

Sarah Nagy

Jennifer Nichols

Amy Oswalt

Brenda Ousley

Fran Ousley

Wendy Pappas

Claire Partain

Bobbi Pennington

Chef Olivier Petit

Dee Dee Phillips

Melodie Phillips

Picola Restaurant

Mona Ponder

Pranzo

Maura Quinn

The Red Bar

Nicole Rewis

Renee Riddle

Frank Robbins

Barbara Roberts

Joy Robertson

Elizabeth Rosenau

Mitzi Rowe

Rutherfords 465

Joanne Ryan

Amy Saxer

Seagar's

Jean Scharnitzky

Sabrina Scherer-
   McLaughlin

Sharon Schinz

Shelley Scholl

Sister Schubert

Chef Priscella Schulze

Ruth Sibbald

Sally Simpson

Bonnie Smith

Butch Smith

Sarah Smith

Hazel Spain

Chef Angie Spensieri

Jennifer Stennett

Chuck Stiles

Barbie Stricklin

Kelley Sumrall

Ann Thomas

Wendy Miller Thomas

Alexis Tibbets

Tony's Pasta by the Sea

Allison Tringas

Anita Turner

Susan Turton

Turton Tea

Lalitha Vadlamani-Simmers

Linda Vardaman

Karly Ann Ward

Lori Ellen Ward

Sandy Watts

Charles West

Lynn West

Kefrin Woodham

Michelle Wright

Index

Beach Appétit

Junior League of the Emerald Coast, Inc.
Post Office Box 531
Fort Walton Beach, Florida 32549
www.jlec.org
850-862-2665

YOUR ORDER	QTY	TOTAL
Beach Appétit at $25.95 per book		$
Postage and handling at $4.25 (1st book) plus $1.00 (each additional book)		$
Florida residents add 6% sales tax per book		$
	TOTAL	$

Name _____

Address _____

City _____ State _____ Zip _____

Telephone _____ Email _____

Method of Payment: | | MasterCard | | VISA
                    | | Check payable to Junior League of the Emerald Coast

Account Number _____ Expiration Date _____

Signature _____

Photocopies will be accepted.